MUSIC MAKING IN AMERICA

Also by Dick Weissman

The Music Business: Career Opportunities and Self-Defense
Audio in Advertising (with Ron Lockhart)
The Folk Music Sourcebook (with Larry Sandberg)

MUSIC MAKING IN AMERICA

Dick Weissman

with photographs

FREDERICK UNGAR PUBLISHING CO.
NEW YORK

Library of Congress Cataloging in Publication Data

Weissman, Dick.
  Music making in America.
  Includes index.   1. Music as a profession.   2. Music and society.
3. Music trade—United States.   4. Music—Economic
aspects.   I. Title.
ML3795.W43   780'.23'73   81-70114
ISBN 0-8044-5977-0   AACR2

CONTENTS

ACKNOWLEDGMENTS

This book has benefited greatly from conversations held over the years with my friends Dan Fox and Harry Tuft. Paul Stewart, founder and curator of the Black America West Foundation in Denver, shared some of his ideas and knowledge about black cowboys. A number of the ideas in the chapter on "The Artist and the Audience" were thoroughly taken apart by Joe Benge, Joe Flexer, and Marie Symes-Grehen at Mitch Podolak's house in Winnipeg at a party after the 1981 Winnipeg Folk Festival. I have wanted to write about Muzak ever since a discussion with Peter Seeger some years ago while we were being attacked by background music on an airplane. Wesley Westbrooks and Mary Flower patiently allowed me to interview them and to interpret their lives. Other valuable discussion and criticisms came from Stith Bennett, Diane Deschanel, Larry Sandberg, and Tasso Harris. I owe a good deal to the patient and persistent editing of Philip Winsor. None of the people who contributed their ideas and time to this book bears any responsibility for my conclusions.

The chapter on "Music as a Part-Time Profession" appeared in a different form in two articles in *Muse*, the newspaper of the Colorado Council on the Arts and Humanities. The chapter on "The Cowboy and His Music" appeared in a somewhat different form in an article published by the Colorado Historical Society. The discussion of Wesley Westbrooks represents my initial re-

viii ACKNOWLEDGMENTS

search funded through a grant from the National Endowment for the Humanities for 1981–82. This research will lead to a book on Wesley's life and music.

In an attempt to avoid stereotyping, I have alternated the use of the pronouns he and she in a random sequence.

This book is dedicated to all musicians everywhere. They deserve more.

INTRODUCTION

A side from the music we listen to voluntarily, we are subjected to an enormous amount of music every day. Our musical soundscape includes radio and television commercials, Muzak in the elevator, and background music in offices or factories; still more music is encountered at shopping malls, on visits to the doctor or dentist, and as background for films and television shows. Millions of Americans play guitar, piano, or other musical instruments in their homes, sing in church and community choirs, or play in community orchestras. Others listen to the music of their choice on home stereos, car radios, portable cassette recorders, and juke boxes as well as at concert halls and nightclubs. Practically all schools have music programs, starting in kindergarten and continuing through college. The Suzuki method of music education has introduced children as young as three years old to the piano, violin, and other instruments.

For all this seeming attention to music, the musician has a difficult time earning a living in our society. Music is considered a luxury item compared to such "real" work as plumbing, mail delivery, or the professions. We frequently honor the end result without considering that the artist who creates or performs music needs to make a living. A typical parental response to a child's interest in pursuing the career in music is the query, "Do you really expect to make a living playing or writing music?'' Organizations regularly ask musicians to do free performances, as though it were an honor for a musician to perform. The same people would never dream of asking an auto mechanic or a doctor to donate professional services. Like most artists, the majority of musicians are rarely eligible for unemployment compensation, because they seldom work for a single employer on a regular basis. Most musicians are in a more or less constant state of unemployment.

The most stable musical work is employment in a major symphony orchestra. The larger orchestras usually have a year-round season, reasonably high minimum wages, and medical benefits. Most symphony musicians never reach the heights of such orchestras as the Cleveland or Boston symphonies but languish in smaller towns, where there are shorter seasons, lower pay scales, and few fringe benefits. Studio musicians and top recitalists earn more money than the symphony players, but their careers involve a greater element of risk. Many musicians do occasional studio work or concert performances, but they are unable to break into the small magic circle of highly paid virtuosos who do the bulk of such work. For the average musician, financial survival is a constant battle, and substantial monetary or aesthetic rewards remain unfulfilled fantasies. The Johnny Cashes, Carly Simons, George Bensons, Isaac Sterns, and Bob Dylans are in the stratosphere, way beyond the reach or even the conception of the struggling journeyman in Dubuque, Iowa.

A number of books have been written about the relationship between music and society, but they do not treat popular music with any respect on the rare occasions when they bother to discuss it.[1] Sociologists of music seem more interested in the structural aspects of music as a profession than in the actual life of the working musician. There is something about modern American sociology that tends to reduce the most interesting characteristics of human beings to a mass of uninteresting data. Too many sociologists have an unintelligible writing style that is more complex than interesting. Most of the useful books about the relationship of music to society deal with specific musicians or particular styles of music. More often than not, these books are written not by sociologists but by perceptive layscholars with some interest in and knowledge of music and the social sciences.[2]

I believe that music is best understood in its own social context, just as a particular song cannot be separated into music without lyrics or vice versa without losing much of its internal meaning. Music making is a process that concerns the relationship between the composer or musician and his or her culture, even if the relationship is one of mutual loathing. Bob Dylan's songwriting, Albert Ayler's anguished saxophone cries, the electronic music of Morton Subotnick, the pop vocal sounds of Eddie Fisher, and the posturing of Mick Jagger are all aspects of twentieth-century America.

I have written seven chapters for this book, and there is a guest chapter by songwriter, record producer, and performer Artie Traum. All the material concerns areas of music and music making that I have pursued over the last twenty years. I am a part-time musician who is also a writer and a teacher. I am a member of the Executive Board of the Denver Musicians' Union and one of the leaders in a reform movement struggling to redefine the function of that union. I have taught music at the high school and college levels, and I have done research on cowboy music and lore for some concert programs with my friend Harry Tuft. My reason for discussing Muzak here is that I have disliked yet been fascinated by the idea of background music for some time. All the chapters in this book, except for the one about the cowboy and his music, relate to the life of professional musicians, including their training, working life, and relationship to American culture.

Today's music is alive with possibilities, unlikely stylistic fusions, and experiments of all kinds. I hope to enrich the reader's grasp of the contemporary music scene and how it has come to be. I want to encourage readers to open their ears to new music of any sort. Most of the exciting new music I have heard is seldom discussed in the media or promoted with any enthusiasm by the corporate structure which controls the sales and distribution of the arts in our society.[3] This is a consequence of the small size of the audience for experimental music. Seeking out the new music should be the task of the critic and listener alike. All of us, laymen and musicians alike, should become listeners.

On the right, Wes Westbrooks as disc jockey at radio station KADX, with Chuck Edwards in the rear running the board, and Steve Steers, now a vice president of United Airlines, on the left, talking to Wes. *Photo by Morgan. Courtesy United Air Lines.*

Mary Flower playing the dobro for friends. *Photo by Diane Deschanel.*

Dick Weissman performing at the Colorado Folk Festival, 1981. *Photo by Diane Deschanel.*

Two cowboys.
*Courtesy of
the Colorado
Historical Society.*

Children performing on Orff instruments, Young Peoples Preparatory
School of Music and Center for the Performing Arts, Boulder, Colorado.
Photo by Diane Deschanel.

Rhythm instruments are fun to play and are effective tools
in teaching music to young children.
Photo by Diane Deschanel.

Fairview High School Marching Band, playing at the
Colorado State Competition in Boulder, 1981.

Artie Traum relaxing in the studio, Woodstock Recording,
Woodstock, New York.

"Black box" display.

Photos by Diane Deschanel.

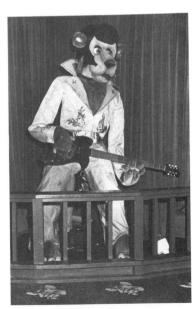

King Leon imitates Elvis Presley
at Chuck E. Cheese pizza chain,
Boulder, Colorado.

Zubin Mehta's debut as Music Director of the New York Philharmonic in Lincoln Center's Avery Fisher Hall, September 14, 1978. *Photo by Marianne Barcellona. Courtesy of the New York Philharmonic Orchestra.*

Street musician plays for spare change, Boulder, Colorado.
Photo by Diane Deschanel.

Mike Seeger,
folklorist and performer
on numerous folk
instruments, Colorado
Folk Festival, 1981.
Photo by Diane Deschanel.

Ian Tyson, well-known
Canadian songwriter
and singer, author
of "Some Day Soon."
Courtesty of Boot Records Ltd.

MUSIC AS A PART-TIME
PROFESSION

About 20 percent of the members of the Musicians' Union
work full-time in music, and another 50 percent do not
work at all.[1] Since many musicians never join the union
or let their membership lapse, there are many more part-time
than full-time players. A small group of full-time professionals
constitute the elite of the music business. They are employed as
soloists in classical music, as studio musicians, or as top-rank
performers of popular music. Altogether, this elite includes fewer
than five thousand musicians. The American Federation of Musicians has a membership of about 280,000, and when we add
to them the nonunion members, this top group represents less
than 2 percent of all the musicians in North America.

Another group of full-time musicians are employed by the
various symphony orchestras. Their income, prestige, and working conditions vary greatly, from a year-round season at a minimum pay scale of over $700 a week to a ten- or twelve-week
season for less than half that amount.

Other musicians do regular work at motels, lounges, nightclubs,
and resorts. Some other musicians are freelancers, who by choice
or accident do not work at a particular job or even in a specific
area but can be found performing in theaters or ice shows, doing
occasional studio work, or playing dances on the weekends. The

life of the freelance player is one of acute insecurity. Each job is but a phone call away, but sometimes the phone doesn't ring.

Each of these approaches to a career in music has certain advantages, such as job security, high wage scales, regularity of work, or quality of music played. Studio work gives a low degree of security outside the very top echelon, but it pays well. It constantly confronts the player with different tasks, and it requires a relatively low number of working hours. On the other hand, studio work demands that the player have a variety of skills, it usually requires that he or she play several instruments with equal facility, and it demands of the musician a very even temperament throughout a broad range of unpredictable circumstances. The studio musician is always for sale to the highest bidder; although the technical abilities required may add to a player's self-esteem, there is a strong element of prostitution in that studio musicians often despise the music they are called upon to perform. Symphony work requires that each player submit to the will of the conductor, and it often involves playing the same repertoire year after year. Job security, salary, and fringe benefits vary with the quality, budget, and reputation of the orchestra and the size of the audience.

The life of the club date or lounge musician is often shrouded in an alcoholic haze, because there is little else to do between shows. Performing in bars requires that the musician keep pace with the latest hits and be willing to fulfill the most outlandish audience requests. I remember seeing a sign in Preservation Hall in New Orleans, where many of the fine older jazz musicians play: "Requests $1.00, Tiger Rag $2.00, When the Saints Go Marching In, $5.00." The sign expresses in a light vein the disparity between the musical tastes of the audience and that of the performing musicians. In other words. if you want to request a tune which bores the musicians, you have to pay extra to have your request fulfilled.

A certain number of musical jobs are obtained through personal contacts or word of mouth rather than ability. In the most competitive pursuits, such as studio work, there is a certain amount of political know-how and protocol involved, working through the hiring bosses, who are called contractors and getting into the studios through the endorsement of players who are already working there.[2] Symphony work is acquired through playing auditions at the player's own expense. For the major symphony jobs, there may be dozens of players auditioning for a single chair. All of them are essentially qualified, but only one can get the job.

The career of the solo recitalist is probably the toughest of all. First the player goes through long and expensive training from a well-known teacher and then makes an obligatory New York debut that he must usually finance himself and that must be favorably reviewed by the critics. The player then enters national and international competitions in an attempt to win a first prize. The winners often receive tours, contracts with top-grade personal managers, and a recording contract with a prestigious record company. A longer and more tortuous route for the recitalist is community concert tours, playing in the smaller towns of North America with other young and little-known musicians. Of course, rising to success in the popular music business is a roulette game with the numbers heavily stacked against the gambler.

Quite a few musicians end up working at another profession or job and play music several nights a week, especially on the weekends. In New Orleans there was a tradition among jazz musicians of holding jobs in a steady trade, such as bricklaying or plastering.[3] The musician who knew a trade could always fall back on it when times were hard or at intervals between musical jobs. Such musicians could also afford to be more selective about the musical jobs that they did take.

The life of the traveling musician has been documented in the memoirs and biographies of everyone from Arthur Rubenstein to Mick Jagger. Top musicians earn a good deal of money on tour, but they lead a life marked by inconsistent eating and sleeping habits, excessive use of drugs and alcohol, and an inability to establish anything but the most transitory relationships. As one passes through the motels and fast-food chains of America, there is a horrible feeling of déjà vu. Many musicians have trouble practicing or writing while on the road, although some seem to be unaffected or even stimulated by travel. Of course, most traveling musicians are not economically successful but must struggle to make it to the next town and the next meal.

When musicians decide to stop traveling, they often arrange to keep a hand in the music business by playing occasional clubs or concerts. There are several reasons why musicians choose to play on a part-time basis. Some people aim to be professional musicians but come to the conclusion that they cannot earn a decent living through music. Others regard music as a sideline to another career. A friend of mine named Art Rosenbaum is an excellent banjo player but earns his living teaching visual arts at the University of Georgia. He has made records, written instruction manuals for the banjo, and even done European tours, but his primary interest is in the visual arts. Some musicians leave the profession for personal reasons. Married musicians may retire because they prefer not to leave their families for long periods of time or to work at night. Some part-time players have made a conscious choice that represents a series of personal or career commitments. The two musicians whom I will discuss here fall into the last category. The lives of Mary Flower and Wesley Westbrooks each unfold an interesting panorama of discoveries, career plans, value conflicts, and personal choices made after a considerable amount of thought.

Mary Flower (her original name was Mary Johnson) is the youngest of six children of a middle-class family in Delphi, Indiana, a small town of under a thousand people. The next youngest sibling is eight years older than Mary, and all the brothers and sisters played instruments in the high school band and sang in the choir. They learned to play and sing by reading music, but Mary's father was a "by ear" musician who sang harmony around the kitchen table with his children. Mary took piano lessons from several teachers when she was about six, but they all refused to continue teaching her when they discovered that she was playing by ear, not from the written music. Later she struggled into the last flute chair in the high school band. At that time she heard some Bob Dylan and Peter, Paul, and Mary records on the radio, and she became interested in the guitar. Her sister Sara was majoring in music therapy at Michigan State and brought home a ukulele during a vacation period. Mary taught herself a few chords, and soon after that her parents bought her a guitar.

Some performances in high school led to a five-girl group called the Hootin Annies. They played at school functions and parties for small sums of money. When Mary entered the University of Indiana in 1967, she encountered all sorts of folk-oriented music, including ragtime, blues, and old-time country music played on banjo, guitar, mandolin, and fiddle by students who came from up and down the East Coast as well as the Midwest. There were several coffeehouses in Bloomington, and it was not long before Mary was singing at open-stage nights and then playing a few professional jobs and teaching guitar at a music store in Bloomington. She was ostensibly a theater major at Indiana, having done some musicals in her high school days, but soon the theater gave way before a serious interest in music.

This interest peaked when Mary was hired to play at a coffeehouse in northern Indiana called Saturday's Child. Dave and Betty Sander ran a very open household and also sang a bit, with Betty playing the twelve-string dobro. They taped all the performances at their coffeehouse. During the course of a dozen jobs there, Mary learned some songs from the tapes and others from the Sanders' extensive record collection.

Although Mary had gone in a different musical direction from anyone else in her family, the whole Johnson family was quite supportive of her musical endeavors. After completing the second year of college, Mary went on a European trip with her sister Sara, trading songs with Parisian street musicians and playing for spare change. When she returned to Bloomington, Mary stayed out of school for a time, working as a maid in a motel and then at an RCA factory, assembling transistors. She returned to college in the spring for one last semester.

For many Americans in the 1960s, college provided an educational forum far removed from the academic experiences of earlier generations. It was a time for testing value systems, of tuning into such things as drugs, sex, bohemian life-styles, and freer ways of thinking and acting. Mary kept a flower on her guitar, and people began to call her Mary Flower, or simply Flower. This was an era of flowers, beads, and peace symbols. To Mary's conservative parents, her jeans and untamed curly hair represented a revolt against the traditional values of neatness and femininity, just as her music represented an uncertain profession in an insecure world. The Johnsons were concerned about their daughter's values and attitudes and could not understand why she would not wear the carefully made clothes her mother had sewed.

By 1970 Mary had formed a duo with a pianist, flautist, and guitar player named Randy Handley. She had met him during one of the Saturday's Child weekends, and they played in bars and pizza parlors for $25 a night each. A year of playing the Bloomington circuit full-time gave them the incentive to try their wings in another place. Sister Sara had moved to Denver, and a friend arranged a contact with a booking agent, who got them a winter of work at a ski resort in Breckenridge, Colorado, about a hundred miles west of Denver. On their days off, Randy and Mary would drive into Denver to check out the local music scene. They played at some open-stage nights in Denver, especially at the Denver Folklore Center. They stayed together for the next few years, but every three or four months Randy would get restless and take off for Indiana or some other place. Mary tried to get solo work and ended up performing at the Denver Folklore Center and briefly at a country and western bar.

Coffeehouses were a folk singer's refuge, a way to get off the street, make musical contacts, and find friends. Mary spent quite a few nights at a coffeehouse called the Zodiac in downtown Denver. Although there was no organized entertainment and musicians were not paid to perform, they would come in off the street to sit around and play. In 1972, David Ferretta, who was then managing the Folklore Center, introduced Mary to Katy

Moffatt, another aspiring musician on the Denver folk scene. Mary and Katy put together a four-piece group with Randy Handley and a bass player named Lon Ephraim. By day Katy would do afternoon cocktail-hour jobs for a Denver booking agent named Mary Mitchell, and nights were spent jamming and rehearsing. Once in a while the quartet got jobs in the mountain ski areas, more often than not resulting in breakdowns of their beat-up automobiles. After six months of this hand-to-mouth existence, Mary Flower proposed to Katy that they "get rid of the other guys" and try to form a duo. Mary Mitchell converted what was supposed to be a solo job for Katy at the Steamboat Village Inn in Steamboat Springs, Colorado, to a duo job. Mary and Katy spent the winter there, working the cocktail hour and practicing most of the night. The job afforded some security, since it included room and board as well as a small salary.

After that job ended, the duo returned to Denver and met a singer named Buck Ford, the son of Tennessee Ernie Ford, and Buck's manager, Patrick West. They signed with Patrick in an attempt to bridge a communications gap with a booking agency called Athena Productions. They felt that Patrick could be an intermediary to Athena and that Athena could get them reasonable bookings. Patrick arranged an audition in New York to play for a weekend coffeehouse circuit, and the duo succeeded in getting six months of bookings along the East Coast. The work was more continuous than lucrative, since Katy's car was a constant expense and there were often three or four days and a lot of miles between jobs. Patrick also arranged for them to open some concerts for the Earl Scruggs Review. Although the money was minimal, he argued that the exposure to large crowds would prove useful. They drove from one job to the next while the review flew. In downtown Philadelphia the police stopped them because they had no rear license plate. A nervous half hour went by and a lot of talking went down before the police finally agreed that the renter's permit was valid.

The Denver music scene expanded when David Ferretta opened a coffeehouse called the Global Village and a folksinger named Jim Ransom started a record company called Biscuit City to record Katy and Mary and several other artists. The first group of artists appeared on a sampler called *Colorado Folk,* recorded on semiprofessional equipment in a tiny studio. The record sold a few thousand copies over a four- or five-year period, but the limited distribution and amateurish quality of the record didn't help the duo. Patrick West went on to a job with a short-lived Denver record company called Crested Butte, and Katy and Mary got to do some free background singing on other people's records. Most of those records were never released.

By 1974 Mary felt that the duo had reached its maximum potential, and she and Katy agreed to go their separate ways.* Mary and Katy both wrote songs, but not enough to constitute a complete repertoire. Mary enjoyed playing and singing but did not really relate to the entertainment aspects of show business. In 1974 she went to work at David Ferretta's new music store.

At about the same time, she met Geoffrey Withers at a hootenanny at the Oxford Hotel in downtown Denver. She and Geoffrey got married in 1975 and had two children in the next three years. Mary thought about giving up music entirely, and she performed only occasionally and began to lose confidence in her musical abilities. The ordeal of ending the duo was depressing, and for a time it seemed that nothing was happening musically in her life. While she was sitting around with three or four women friends one day, the idea came of forming a female performing group called the Motherfolkers. The group performed during International Women's Week and worked at various jobs for the next six years. For a time it appeared that they would make a record for a national label, but recently this fell through. The future of the Motherfolkers is uncertain, but they caused quite a stir in the Denver music community because there were so many competent women musicians represented in the group in so many roles. There were multiinstrumentalists, a fine banjo soloist, numerous singer-songwriters, and an excellent comedian.

* Katy went on to do two solo records for Columbia, but they didn't sell well, and she has continued her musical career in Los Angeles.

In 1978 Mary put a trio together called Sweet Georgia Brown. They performed swing-oriented music of the 1930s and 1940s, working together regularly for about a year. The group provided a welcome respite from the responsibilities of home and family, but a brief experience in the recording studio indicated that they had no real future together. The pressures of a recording situation made the trio realize that they were not musically or personally compatible.

Mary's husband, Geoffrey Withers, has a B.A. in music from the University of Denver. After three years as manager of the Denver Folklore Center, he abandoned a career in music, and he now works for the state of Colorado as a water and sewer consultant for the Council on Governments. Mary has developed her career as a freelance musician, playing with a number of different bands and working as a soloist while continuing to write songs. In the Withers household, it is the husband who has pretty much given up his musical career, although not his interest in music. Mary still works bar gigs or concerts, averaging about two weekends of work each month. She also does studio work in Denver as a singer and dobro and guitar player.

Mary is more cautious today than she was ten years ago about jumping into new groups or musical commitments. She feels that it is impractical to try to support her family as a musician, and she doesn't like being away from her children. She enjoys the variety and challenge of working with different bands, even though it is sometimes distracting to shift musical gears so often. She hopes to play music forever, but not as a full-time career. In her opinion, women need a certain amount of domesticity. She is comfortable with her musical and personal life. Her major musical ambition is to do a solo record and to play at major summer music festivals, where she would be stimulated by the experience of meeting and performing with other musicians. Performing is a good way of earning some extra money for the family budget rather than a full-time career.

I feel that Mary Flower has made a sensible adjustment to the situation of being a wife and mother without giving up her musical

identity or interests. Her solution might prove practical for many
people, especially women in similar circumstances.[4]

Wesley Westbrooks could hardly have come from a more different background than Mary Flower, and yet in many ways he
has wound up in a similar position. Wesley was born into a black
family in Arkadelphia, Arkansas, in 1920, one of four children.
His father was a cook at a nearby white college and played drums.
All the musicians Wesley knew in Arkansas were self-taught, except for a few church pianists who had learned to play by reading
music. Wes's earliest musical mentor was a self-taught musical
jack-of-all-trades named Doodley Williams. Doodley played any
number of musical instruments, and although he never had any
money, he always seemed to be able to figure out some way to
get instruments.[5] As a young boy, Wes played drums in Arkadelphia and nearby towns, working his first job when the drummer who had been hired became too drunk to play. At age
fourteen, Wes moved to Kansas City, Kansas. He stayed there
through high school, singing and playing trumpet in the school
music program. He also sang and played drums at many informal
sessions at his house or the houses of friends.

Wesley was a teenager in the heyday of Kansas City jazz, when
musicians such as Lester Young, Jay McShann, and the young
Charlie Parker were cutting their musical teeth at jam sessions
in nightclubs and after-hours joints in Kansas City, Missouri.
Wesley got to attend some of these sessions and meet many
Kansas City jazzmen. During high school he earned an occasional
dollar playing drums and singing at small clubs or school
functions.

Wes bought his first trumpet at Sam's Pawnshop in Kansas
City, Kansas. It cost $12, which he paid off on time, and a mouth-
piece for the horn cost another $1.75. It was not until 1939, after
his high school graduation, that he got a reasonable mouthpiece,
a Bouchet. After graduation he jobbed around, working as a
drummer in the Kansas City area. Around 1941, Wes realized
that he would be drafted to serve in the armed forces, and so

he took a series of trips to and from Chicago in an attempt to delay the process. In 1942 he was drafted and went to Fort Leavenworth, Kansas, and then to Alabama before being shipped to north Africa and Italy, where he spent the rest of World War II.

World War II put Wesley Westbrooks through many personal and psychological changes. As a young black man raised in the totally segregated environment of rural Arkansas and the mostly segregated world of Kansas City, he had made little or no contact with the world outside the ghetto. In north Africa and Italy, Wesley met white people who knew and cared about black music, and he took lessons at a music school in Florence, discovering that some of the Italians seemed to care more about his musical roots than he did.

When Wes's company was demobilized, one of the white officers (all the officers in the company were white, and all the regular soliders were black) announced to the company that they were eligible to go to school under the GI Bill, but he doubted that any of them would be smart enough to take advantage of the opportunity. Wes quickly decided that he would use that opportunity. Shortly after his discharge from the Army, he joined a friend named LH on a trip to California. Wes played trumpet in a number of groups around Sacramento and San Francisco for about eight months. He heard the fine bebop trumpeter Howard McGhee and tried to imitate his style, and he played trumpet behind blues singers Pee Wee Crayton and Saunders King. Wes also got to hang out with the members of the Billy Eckstine bebop band, one of the earliest and best big bands that used progressive jazz arrangements in the postwar bebop style. Wes got to sit in on a number of their rehearsals and even to play occasional jobs with them.

Through the influence of two friends, he went to Chicago and enrolled at the Midwestern Conservatory of Music. For two years he studied classical playing and writing styles, supported by the GI Bill, and played occasionally to supplement his income. Some of Wes's Kansas City friends, such as the fine alto saxophone player John Jackson, felt that Wes was too "bookish," that his playing was too stiff. Wes's decision to go to school was largely motivated by his attempt to come to terms with the complex bebop styles that had emerged while he was in the service.

After two years at Midwestern, Wes switched over to the Cosmopolitan Conservatory in Chicago for another year. He made some futile attempts to study the Schillinger arranging method, a mathematically oriented and complicated system of orchestration that he had encountered through an arranger named Jerry Valentine. Jerry had been working with the Billy Eckstine band in California when Wes was out there and had let Wes sit in on a number of rehearsals and a few jobs.

By this time, Wes began to feel the need for a challenge, and the place for that was obviously New York. He realized that in the Kansas City and Chicago areas he was getting jobs not because he was a good player but because he was from Kansas City and had a good social relationship with many of the musicians of that city. New York was the center of the jazz world, and Wes eased his way there, first going to Philadelphia for a few months and then to Washington, D.C. While in Washington, he played briefly with the baritone sax player Leo Parker and took music classes at Howard University. Howard was a strict school attended by representatives of the black bourgeoisie. It was obvious that Wes did not fit into that scene, and he finally made his way to New York City.

From 1950 to 1951 Wes lived the life of the New York bebopper, scrounging occasional menial jobs, spending a couple of months "living on the stick," spending nights on the subway, and sleeping in friends' apartments during the day. He acquired a heroin habit, which was almost an obligatory part of the bebop experience of that time. He made a living through his music jobs and by playing con games with white tourists in Harlem. Fats Navarro, the trumpet player, lived across the street from Wes on Fifth Avenue, and he gave Wes some playing tips. When Fats died from tuberculosis aggravated by drug abuse, Wes moved uptown to the Bronx and tried to lessen his dependence on drugs. He enrolled at the Music Conservatory of the Bronx, studying trumpet and arranging for a year and a half. In 1952, Wes reached the point where he felt he had to leave New York, and he wanted to end his drug habit entirely. He thought about going to the federal narcotic rehabilitation center in Lexington, Kentucky, but ended up kicking the habit on his own.

All the time he was studying music, Wes had no interest in getting a college degree. He was simply trying to learn as much about music as he could at each school. Gradually his interests turned more to arranging and composing than playing. Wes's GI Bill school benefits had run out, but he heard that he could get a music scholarship at the University of Arkansas at Pine Bluff if he would agree to play in the school band. From 1952 to 1953 he attended school there, playing in the college band and in smaller ensembles that worked professionally when the big band was not playing. The big band played quite a few arrangements purchased from music publishers, arrangements used by bands such as the Stan Kenton orchestra. Wes met a bass player named Jamil Nasser, and he and Wes wrote some arrangements for the band and sometimes conducted it. The school band toured Texas, Louisiana, and Arkansas, and the school received the money for these performances. The arrangements that Wes had written were the first formal musical arrangements he had ever done, and he enjoyed the stimulation of writing for the band. In the summer, Wes and some of the other Pine Bluff students put together a small combo and worked clubs in the Galesburg, Illinois, area.

In summer 1952, Wes married a Kansas City high school classmate, Alleze Thompson. A year later Wes quit school and moved to Kansas City, where Alleze had a job working for the Internal Revenue Service. Shortly after they married, Alleze got a transfer to the Air Force accounting office in Denver and went there to get an apartment. Several weeks later, Wes went to Denver and got a job as a porter for the Union Pacific Railroad. After a brief weekend visit to Kansas City, he decided that if he really wanted to travel, he should get a job working for the airlines because

traveling by railroad took too much time. He went to work cleaning airplanes for United Airlines in 1955 and has used his travel
privileges to keep up with his friends' musical endeavors.

One day while he was practicing trumpet in his apartment, the
landlord asked him to stop because it was disturbing him. Wes
took the trumpet to a Denver pawnshop and has never retrieved
it or played trumpet since. He decided that there was no point
continuing to play music when it would not support a reasonable
life-style. During the next few years Wes worked as a choral
director for a city youth program and managed to stay on top
of the latest music trends with the help of a friend named Austin
Miller, who worked for a local record distributor. Wes hung
around with the local musicians, who included guitarist Bob Gray
who was an old Army buddy, and the pianist Cedar Walton, then
a music student at the University of Denver. With three partners,
Wes opened an after-hours spot called the Red Carpet. It was
a place where musicians would come after finishing their jobs to
jam with other musicians, and it lasted a couple of years.

In the twenty-six years Wes Westbrooks has lived in Denver,
he has been on the radio as a disc jockey almost the entire time.
First he co-hosted a gospel music show on Sunday mornings.
It started out as a half-hour show and then went to an hour and
a half before an evening program was added. About two years
ago the radio station changed its format, and Wes left to start a
blues show on a local jazz station. Wes's involvement with gospel
music came about through a friend in Los Angeles who turned
him on to a hot new gospel group called the Staples Singers in
the mid-1950s. Their style was something of a departure from
the male quartet styles that had previously dominated gospel
music. Using his flying privileges as a United employee, Wes flew
out to Chicago and met Roebuck Staples, the leader of the group.
Wes wrote a number of gospel songs for which Staples supplied
titles and song ideas, and a Denver collaborator named Harriet
Rice did some of the lyrics. Sometimes Wes wrote both the words
and the music. Two of Wes's songs, "You Don't Knock" and
"Hear My Call Here," were picked up and recorded by well-

known white groups. "You Don't Knock" was recorded by the Kingston Trio. All the Trio's albums sold in the hundreds of thousands, and this resulted in the most money Wes has ever made in the music business. "Hear My Call Here" was recorded by the English group the Pentangle in a version that Wesley feels conveys almost exactly what he had in mind.

In several instances Wes never received any credit or money for his songs, because he never bothered to execute the contracts that Staples asked him to sign. When Wes did sign contracts, Staples usually was given credit as the co-author. In many instances Staples suggested song topics or titles. Some of Wes's friends feel that Staples's contributions to the songs were relatively insignificant. The practice of an artist cutting himself in on a song copyright was quite common in the music business at that time, and is not unknown today. It is also possible that the lack of composer credits for Wes reflects administrative inefficiency on the part of whoever prepared the credits. In any case Staples made at least some contributions to the songs. Wes is philosophical about this, although he lost quite a bit of money when one of these songs, "Why Am I Treated So Bad?" became a big hit for Cannonball Adderley. Since Wes did not depend on music as his primary source of income, he was able to use music as an outlet for his feelings and not to worry about the economics of musical success. Although he understands that he may have erred, at least from an accountant's point of view, he does not care much.

Wes's other main musical activity in Denver is working as a songwriter and musical arranger with a gospel-oriented group called Roots and Branches. They provided an excellent outlet for Wes's songs, but since they are currently unrecorded and not widely known outside Denver, there have been some frustrations in working with them as well. Cliff Young, who sings and plays piano in the group, is an excellent singer and a fine interpreter of Wes's music; if Roots and Branches play to a broader audience, it will be an opportunity for Wes to carry his music to more people. As Wes approaches retirement age at United, he is interested in doing musical work with children in some sort of teaching capacity.*

In examining the careers of Mary Flower and Wesley Westbrooks, we can see quite a few common elements and attitudes, despite the differences in age, musical style, and general outlook. Both used college as a vehicle for finding out about the world and about music rather than as an investment in job security through a degree program. Both spent time playing music as a full-time occupation, and neither found the experience gratifying. Marriage and raising a family intensified the insecurity of the music business, and so both left music as a career after marriage. Both live in Denver, where each has contributed quite a bit to the musical community, Wes as an arranger, composer, and disc jockey, and Mary as a performing musician and songwriter.

Although each has experienced a variety of musical frustrations through a lack of performing opportunities over the years and the limited economic returns from the music business, both Wes and Mary are better off than many musicians who are part-time workers but persist in the illusion that they have found a full-time occupation in music. Perhaps some day both will get a chance to teach their music to children, although at the present time the school system is not structured to make use of that sort of valuable community resource. In any case, they have retained their love for music and their enthusiasm for it. These attitudes are often lacking in the world of the full-time professional musician.[6]

---

* Wesley Westbrooks will never have the opportunity to fulfill the musical aspirations of his retirement years because he died December 27, 1981, after a six-month battle with cancer. It is my sincere desire that his musical legacy be carried on through the singing of Cliff Young, my own forthcoming biography, and the memories, songs, and dreams of his family and friends.

CONFESSIONS OF AN UNREPENTANT BANJO PLAYER

When I was growing up, I did not plan to become a musician. I took piano lessons for about seven years, starting at age seven. I played classical music, and the lessons consisted entirely of reading music and practicing scales and simple technical exercises. I exhibited talent for music and had some inclination to play, but I didn't show much improvement after the first two or three years of lessons. In elementary school, my interests turned more to softball and football, but I usually managed to practice thirty to sixty minutes a day.

When I was thirteen years old, in 1948, I went to the Progressive Party convention in Philadelphia and saw Pete Seeger play the banjo. I was fascinated by his music. I had never heard any banjo music except what is played in Philadelphia during the annual New Year's Day Mummers' Parade, and music had never interested me. I did not know that the five-string banjo was a different instrument from the tenor and plectrum banjos that were used in the parade or that the techniques for playing the five-string were quite different from the techniques the mummers used.

Shortly after the convention ended, I discovered an army-navy surplus store in downtown Philadelphia that was selling discontinued 78 RPM records. Among the selections offered was a group of records on the Disc label featuring such musicians as Pete Seeger, Woody Guthrie, and the bluesmen Brownie McGhee, Sonny Terry, and Lonnie Johnson. I came from a middle-class Jewish family; my father was a hospital superintendent and my mother an ex-school teacher. For some reason, I could identify equally with blues music from the Afro-American fold tradition and the songs from the southern Appalachian mountains that stemmed from the Anglo-Saxon heritage of Appalachia. No one I knew at my middle-class high school, Central High, had any interest in this music, and so I got to feel that folk music was something special to me. My identification with both major streams of the American folk song tradition has remained strong to this day.

By the time I was a sophomore in high school, I had lost interest in the piano. I was interested in the social sciences and literature and in playing table tennis. I started to compete in tournaments, including several in New York City. Some of my competitors introduced me to the pleasures of modern jazz. This was around 1950, and the records my friends played for me featured such jazz players as Charlie Parker and Thelonious Monk. Thanks to my New York friends, my enthusiasm for jazz developed concurrently with my increasing interest in American folk music. I never developed much of an interest in popular music at that time except for six months spent listening to the hits of the day. The hit makers were people like Eddie Fisher and Doris Day, and I did not identify with them.

Most of my high school classmates went on to college. I didn't have any definite plans, and so I took a year off to think, work, and play table tennis tournaments. On the back of one of the Pete Seeger albums I read about his book *How to Play the Five String Banjo*. I sent for the book and then went out to a pawnshop and bought a banjo, as the book suggested. I already could read music, and I thought it would be fairly easy to learn to play the banjo. When I tried to tune the banjo to the proper piano notes, I immediately broke two strings. I gave up and put the instrument in the closet.

About six months after I graduated from high school I bought Pete Seeger's first long-playing record, *Darling Corey*. Seeger sang a number of songs and played a medley of banjo tunes on this record. To this day it is the only record that I have ever literally worn out. I used to play it every day before I went to work, after I came home, and before I went to bed. I don't know where the record took me, but I remember being happy to go along for the ride.

I spent six months running a mimeograph machine in a Philadelphia department store, and that was enough to convince me that I wanted to go to college. I spent the next six months floating from one job to another, playing in table tennis tournaments, and buying old blues records. I then enrolled in Goddard College, a progressive school in Plainfield, Vermont, that did not give marks or tests.

I arrived at Goddard with a stack of folk and jazz records. The first night at school I attended a party at which an ex-student played the banjo. She was a reasonably good player, but I couldn't see any relationship between what she was doing and what I had heard on Seeger's records. I also met a student named Burrill Crohn, who asked if I could play any musical instruments. Before I knew it, he had persuaded me to attempt some Dixieland and blues piano while he played the trumpet. Somewhere in the process of listening to jazz, I had picked up a couple of books about blues piano, and I could play some very elementary blues piano. Over the next two years we played together quite often, and I even wrote a blues lamenting his charms, something to the effect of: "Baby, if you love me, why did you go home with Burrill Crohn? All night I was drinking beer, and waiting for you at my home. . . ."

I made friends with another student named Lil Blos. She played the banjo simply but quite well, and she offered to teach me how to play. I brought my banjo back to school after the Thanksgiving vacation, and she gave me some lessons. This was probably the most significant event of my college career. I practiced the banjo for hours: in my room, in front of the campus community center, or in a special place in the woods. It may have driven people crazy, but Goddard was a very accepting place, and no one complained.

Everything I was playing was learned by ear or from watching other players. I played records over and over again in an attempt to figure out what the musicians were doing. Occasionally I used Seeger's book as a theoretical background to what Lil was showing me. All of my banjo playing and most of the piano playing I did with Burrill was in a totally different realm from what I had learned through my piano lessons.

By my sophomore year, Lil had left Goddard and I was on my own. I knew two or three guitar players with whom I could play and exchange ideas, but essentially I was solidifying what I already knew about the banjo. I picked up a cheap guitar in payment for a ping pong gambling debt and taught myself a few guitar chords as well. I continued to practice incessantly and began to play at parties.

The Goddard program obligated students to work during January and February at whatever jobs were available. In my sophomore year, I got a job working at the New York Public Library. At the end of January I developed herpes virus in my left eye and had to go home to Philadelphia. I took atropine eye drops that were so powerful that I couldn't focus my left eye for six weeks. The only thing I could do was play the radio and the banjo. During this six-week period I became a reasonably decent banjo player because I spent so much time and energy practicing without distractions.

For my junior year I decided to study elsewhere, because Goddard was a very small school. I spent the fall at the New School for Social Research in New York and the spring semester at the University of New Mexico. As part of my academic program in New York, I studied banjo and guitar with Jerry Silverman, a well-known folk guitarist. He was also a reasonably good banjo player, and he taught me to play chords up the neck. Jerry succeeded in turning some of my attention to the technical and theoretical aspects of the instrument. In New Mexico I met an outstanding banjoist named Stu Jamieson. I spent two long evenings at Stu's house and watched him play mountain banjo styles. Stu had spent quite a bit of time in Kentucky with a famous player named Rufus Crisp, who played the banjo in a number of different tunings. Stu's playing was clean and precise, and he provided me with a lot of inspiration. He lived on a mountain overlooking Albuquerque, working as an engineer for the Sandia Corporation. Because he did not depend on music for a livelihood, Stuart played only the music that he enjoyed.

I returned to Goddard for my senior year. Another student and I decided to do a folk concert as part of graduation week. I felt that I wanted to perform something special, and I spent a good part of the late fall and winter thinking about what I could play that would have some special meaning for me and would also appeal to my classmates. I chose a topic for my senior thesis that blended my interests in music and the social sciences. I chose to write about Leadbelly, the black folk singer. I wanted to analyze the lyrics of his songs and the relationship between his life and his music.

If I had gone to college in the present era, my major field would have been described as American or black studies, but since nothing of this sort was available to me, I thought of myself as majoring in the social sciences. For academic purposes, this translated into a sociology major, even though I had taken only two sociology courses during my undergraduate career.

During the winter work period, I gave out toothpaste samples in New York and did some research for my thesis. A man named Bob Harris who ran a small record store and folk record company called Stinson Records told me about a guitarist and singer named Gary Davis. Gary played every Tuesday night at Tiny Ledbetter's apartment on East Tenth Street. Gary Davis was a blind street singer and preacher who made his living in Harlem, playing music and collecting coins in a tin cup. I went down to Tiny's apartment a half a dozen times, listening to Gary's singing sermons and sometimes trying to play banjo with him. He used an unorthodox system of fingering with the left hand; when I played with him,

I had to listen rather than try to follow his fingering patterns. This made me very nervous, because I literally did not know what I was doing, but it also resulted in my playing beyond my abilities. I met quite a few fine musicians during these six weeks, including Erik Darling, Woody Guthrie, and John Gibbon. Tiny Ledbetter was Leadbelly's niece, and through her I met Martha Ledbetter, his widow, and some other musicians. I cannot overestimate the influence that these sessions had on me. I got totally caught up in the music. Gary played and sang blues songs with religious lyrics. All the musicians listened to him carefully and added little musical codas to his speeches. I didn't realize it at the time, but this was the first inkling I had that I could devote my life to a career in music.

When I returned to Goddard in March, I decided to write a suite for the banjo. It was in five parts, including an opening theme, a slow movement, a song, a blues, and a recapitulation of the whole piece. I called it "A Day In The Kentucky Mountains" and practiced it for hours, working out all the parts. It included specific themes and extended improvisations, and most of it was written outdoors in the Vermont woods. When we did our graduation concert, people seemed to like the suite, but they didn't know what to make of it. I felt good about it because after three years of playing the banjo, I had begun to develop my own voice on the instrument.

During my senior year at Goddard, I played my first professional music job, picking banjo at a square dance in East Bethel, Vermont, with a group called Emerson Lang's Green Mountain Volunteers. All I can remember from that job is a set of very sore fingers from hours of playing and a boy and a girl dancing together who seemed very much in love.

The summer after my graduation I went out to Yellowstone National Park, where I had worked the previous summer selling fishing trips. I had gotten the same job again, together with a job for a girl I was going with. The Yellowstone Park Company paid $25 each for our fare, and we decided to hitchhike the rest of the way. We got off in Nebraska and waited five hours for a ride which never came. It turned out that there had been a gory hitchhiker murder there the preceding day, and no one was in the mood to pick up riders. Carol promptly got an attack of tonsilitis. She stayed at a local hotel, while I slept out in a Nebraska field during a horrible lightning storm, which scared me so badly that I crawled into a prefabricated doghouse and stayed there all night. We got another bus to Cheyenne, where Carol ended up in the hospital with her tonsilitis, and I ended up hitchhiking to Yellowstone after a brief bus ride to Rawlins, Wyoming.

About one hundred fifty miles from the park, I got stuck in Dubois, Wyoming, when a cowboy in a pickup truck saw me standing on the main street with a banjo case. He drove around the block and asked me if I'd like to work that night. I agreed, and he promptly took me to the local restaurant, where two fairly attractive girls proceeded to half smother him to death while I looked on in amazement. He had been a bass player on a Grand Ole Opry tour with a singer named T. Texas Tyler and had returned home to Dubois, where he did some sort of ranching. My new friend outfitted me in a western shirt, French cuffs, and boots, and we went to the local bar, which was a long hall with a large dance floor that looked like something out of a western movie set.

When my friend Charley played bass, I played guitar, using his guitar; when he played guitar, I played banjo. The rest of the band consisted of an old tenor banjo player and a drummer. As the evening progressed, hundreds of people swarmed onto the dance floor, and a group of clearly under-age Indians managed to get into the bar. One of them staggered up to the bandstand and began to sing unaccompanied Cree lullabies. I thought they were great, but most of the Anglos in the audience hated them and forced him off the bandstand. Fortunately, his friends were preoccupied with their own affairs, and the violence that was in the air never erupted. At the end of the night, Charley drove me to his house and gave me $5 for playing about five hours instead of the $15 he had promised. He said that the bartender wouldn't give him any more money. I didn't argue. I figured that I had earned the equivalent of several years of experience in playing bars.

I spent the next five years in New York City. I started a Master's program in sociology at Columbia University. My parents paid my tuition, but I paid for all my living expenses by teaching banjo and guitar and doing occasional playing jobs. Through Bob Harris, I made my first recording for Stinson Records, accompanying a West Indian folk singer named Dick Silvera. He had a classically trained voice and a repertoire that included some interesting Ohio River songs. I think I earned $50 for playing banjo and guitar on the album. I was not a member of the Musicians' Union at that time, but shortly thereafter I got a chance to do an album called *Banjos, Banjos, and More Banjos,* with Billy Faier and Eric Weissberg. Eric became quite famous years later through his hit recording of "Dueling Banjos," which he also played in the movie *Deliverance.* In order to record for Riverside Records, the company that did the banjo album, I had to join the Musicians' Union. The New York local of that union has a residency requirement and an audition procedure. The audition consists of reading music; if you don't want to or can't read music, you simply tell them that you sing and accompany yourself. I didn't care to take the test, and so I opted for the second alternative. The examiner asked my to play for him, and so I sang and played an old mountain song called "Pretty Polly." After he had heard about half a verse, he asked me to stop, and he passed me. I was disappointed, because I had psyched myself up to play for ten or fifteen minutes.

Gradually my name became known to people in the New York studio world, and I got to do recordings and commercials. This work came from two different sources. As an instrumentalist and folk singer, I spent quite a bit of time in Greenwich Village and met singers who needed additional accompaniment. Other work came through word of mouth among arrangers, composers, and studio guitarists. Studio work is a sort of closed club; to gain entrance, you have to prove that you are stable and reliable as well as a good player. I met a number of studio guitarists through hanging out at a midtown guitar shop called Eddie Bell's. Eddie did repairs for a number of the top studio guitarists, who often would go there between recording sessions to socialize and exchange musical ideas and gossip. I enjoyed the atmosphere and music at the shop, and I became friendly with Paula and Eddie Bell, who took a sort of parental interest in my activities.*

Paula advised me to stay away from music as a career, but she or Eddie nevertheless recommended me for some studio work. Most of the studio guitarists also played tenor banjo and mandolin, but they avoided the five-string banjo because of its different tuning and the special technique required to play it. My first commercial was arranged and conducted by Raymond Scott, who had been the bandleader on the *Lucky Strike Hit Parade* radio and television shows. I was extremely nervous but managed to get through the banjo part reasonably well. It was simply a bunch of chords, complicated by the fact that I had to transpose the part from one key to another. The guitarists on the date were Barry Galbraith and Al Caiola, two of the top players in New York. During a break, I showed them a folk style of guitar called finger picking. This was in 1958, and I don't think either of them had ever seen anyone play in that style before. Later, when some friends told me how good these players were, I was embarrassed to have played guitar for them.

Because of my seven years of piano lessons, I could read music for banjo and guitar, but compared to the top studio guitarists in New York, my knowledge of music was elementary. The five-string banjo was an unfamiliar instrument to most arrangers and composers; consequently, they generally allowed me to make up my own parts. This was just as well, because my ability to sight-read music lagged below my playing level. As I began to get more recording work, I gradually made the transition from graduate student to professional musician. I had no clear idea about how I would make a living over a long period of time, but I was single and felt that I could be self-supporting by playing and teaching

* The shop continues today under different ownership at another location.

music. It was clear that I would never be a sociologist, and I had never made any effort to realize my childhood fantasy of being a writer. I had become a musician through the elimination of other options.

I began to search for a sensible vehicle to perform music, given the fact that I was basically a musician who also sang rather than a singer who also played. My first singing partner was Happy Traum, a good guitarist with a warm stage manner and an average singing voice. I lacked the self-confidence to perform alone because I was extremely self-conscious and was never confident that my music could interest an audience. After Happy and I drifted apart, I teamed up with an excellent singer named Pat Foster. We recorded three albums, two of which were released. Pat was truly a golden-voiced singer, and a rather unusual person. He didn't perform well in public because his personal magnetism was short-circuited by a rather strong streak of hostility. The experience I acquired accompanying Pat proved invaluable. Pat played a simple rhythm guitar, and he relied on me to provide instrumental color and texture. We did very little performing, although we made one hitchhiking trip to New England, picking up a job in Harriman, New York, entertaining a group of businessmen at a summer management workshop.

Pat was quite a magnetic character, especially for women. He delighted in regaling me with stories of his sexual adventures, particularly if he thought that I was attracted to the woman in question. I remember that he lived with a woman named Delores in the West Sixties in New York. One day she decided to throw him out, and he developed an acute attack of amnesia, claiming that he couldn't remember his name, his character, or anything else. I thought that he was acting, but he did such a good job that the police refused to take him away from Delores's apartment, and he earned a few more days of free rent while figuring out where to go next. The last time I saw Pat was around 1962, when I was playing at the Hungry I in San Francisco. He was wandering around the streets of North Beach, probably working out some con scheme to find a place to stay and was most likely about to charm a woman into supporting him.

One of my more amusing experiences with Pat occurred while we were doing an album of talking blues for a record company called Esoteric/Counterpoint. Talking blues are songs in a simple musical format that are talked in a sort of singsong style rather than sung. They are usually somewhat humorous; the master of the form was Woody Guthrie, who wrote dozens of them. We decided to write one, too, but we told Bill Fox, the owner of the company, that Pat had collected the song in California. We patched the song together from some of Pat's experiences and fantasies and from a day I had spent picking blueberries in southern New Jersey. Bill never suspected that we had written the song, and some scholarly analysis of the song appears in a book by Kenneth Allsop, *Hard Travellin'*.[1] In those days a legitimate folk singer didn't write songs, unless his name was Woody Guthrie!

During that same summer of 1958, I played on two network television shows. One was an NBC special called *The Ragtime Years,* and the other was an ABC Labor Day show. I got the first job through my friend Israel Young, who had started the Folklore Center, a folk music supply store in New York. I played banjo for about five seconds, accompanying a folk singer named Robin Roberts, who sang a song illustrating the folk roots of ragtime. I suggested that my friend Eric Weissberg play fiddle with us, and he in turn recommended me for the Labor Day show. The ragtime show involved a week of rehearsals and tapings and featured many fine musicians, including the great pianist Eubie Blake, and Hoagy Carmichael, the host of the show. This was my first contact with an expensive musical extravaganza.

Many of the rehearsals and taping for *The Ragtime Years* were boring; even though I was playing for only half a minute, I was compelled to be there for the entire show. One day Hoagy Carmichael was having a very bad time reciting his lines without any flubs. As he missed another line, Eric leaned over to me and said, "Do you think in twenty years they'll do a show about us and call it *The Folk Years?*" I broke out in laughter just as Hoagy blew his line. Carmichael turned to me and proceeded to tell me what a jerk I was, and did I think I could do any better than he could? I turned beet red and mumbled that I wasn't laughing at him. I'm sure he didn't believe me.

Israel Young, the proprietor of the New York Folklore Center, was hired to co-manage a night club in Greenwich Village called Gerde's Folk City, and he asked me to be the opening act for Brownie McGhee and Sonny Terry. I played with them for three weeks, sitting in during the last show of the evening, adding my banjo to their guitar and harmonica. My roommates and I also hosted two all-night parties which Brownie and Sonny attended, along with John Lee Hooker and every young blues aficionado in New York.

The music I enjoyed most at this point was music that reflected some sort of folk roots. I heartily disliked commercial music, although this did not prevent me from accepting studio work of all kinds. Studio musicians tend to develop a strong layer of cynicism and practicality, based on the knowledge that their work pays well and never lasts very long.

One person who influenced my musical attitudes was Hedy West. Hedy was a banjoist, singer, flautist, artist, and drama student. In 1959, she and I and two other musicians were picked to form what may have been the world's first and worst folk rock group. It was called The Citizens, and it was put together by two Tin Pan Alley songwriters named Lou Stallman and Sid Jacobson to record an album of songs they had written about New York City. I played banjo and guitar and sang, Hedy sang and played the flute, and Lenny Levine sang and played guitar. The fourth singer, Al Wenger, was removed from the group during rehearsals, and Stallman himself sang on the record. We recorded for Laurie Records, a small but successful rock and roll label that had recorded Dion and the Belmonts and the Chiffons.

The Citizens represented my first real foray into commercial music. The music was not well written or interesting, and it turned out not to be commercially successful. The rehearsals were end-less before we finally got into the recording studio. I also barely escaped signing a management and recording contract with Stall-man and Jacobson that would have put me behind the eight ball later. Laurie eventually released the records in a very perfunctory way, and they faded into oblivion.

It was 1960, and I was twenty-five years old. I had been playing music full-time for about three years and supplementing my in-come by giving lessons. The music that I enjoyed most was southern mountain music and old blues. I wasn't interested in the successful folk singers of the time, such as Joan Baez. I felt that they were too involved in themselves and the commercial aspects of music. I use Baez as an example because she was one of the few successful folk singers who was interested in main-taining some authenticity of spirit in her performances. I was so alienated from the commercial world that she seemed commercial to me. I began to worry about what I would be doing to make a living ten years from 1960. I enjoyed playing music, I was living with two friends in a $105 a month seven-room apartment, and my needs were relatively modest.

Through Israel Young, I met a singer and songwriter named John Phillips. He was the leader of a male vocal quartet called the Smoothies. They sang in a jazzy Four Freshmen–Hi Los style of harmony, but they hadn't succeeded in making any hit records. They wanted to try their hand at folk-pop music, and they were looking for guidance on folk styles. I went to a couple of their rehearsals, and we worked out a few musical arrangements. I suggested that we add Eric Weissberg to the band for the re-cording. They accepted that idea, and the recording date featured a blend of written arrangements played by some top studio play-ers, such as guitarist Don Arnone, and Eric and I playing the folk-style solos. One thing led to another, and John and I started to hang out together, going to parties and playing music. John and Scott Mackenzie, one of his singing partners from the Smoothies, decided to quit the Smoothies, and they asked me to join them in starting a new pop-folk group.

Given my orientation, this went against all my musical ideas. On the other hand, I had succeeded in ignoring such factors when I played with The Citizens. I was excited at the idea of traveling around the country, meeting new people, trying to make some hit records, and earning a lot of money. I felt that I had lived in New York long enough. It was time to try something new. I made a commitment to try the group for three years, save $100,000, and then move to Colorado and go to music school. We agreed to start the group, and John and Scott went to Windsor, Ontario, to play their last job with the Smoothies while I went to Los Angeles to play with an international folk singer named Martha Schlamme at a club called the Ash Grove.

I drove from Philadelphia to Denver with my old friend Harry Tuft in a driveaway car and took the Santa Fe Railroad train the "Super Chief" to Los Angeles from there. At the Ash Grove, I opened the show, followed by a theatrical review called *Jewels by Feiffer,* that acted out some Jules Feiffer cartoons. Then Martha came on and closed the show, accompanied by me. I was very excited about playing at the Ash Grove and meeting the people in the Los Angeles folk scene. Playing for Martha was stimulating because she used written arrangements with quite a few of the guitar parts written out precisely. Although I could read music, I was a bit lazy about it and was used to interpreting music in any way I felt was appropriate. Martha was a very disciplined performer and didn't let me get away with this attitude. I did quite a bit of practicing and mastered most of the arrangements.

My own performances did not go as smoothly. I was not used to talking to the audience, and I felt embarrassed and ill at ease. Frank Mahoney, one of the actors in the company, took pity on me and showed me how to get the audience to relax. He taught me that it was possible for me to be funny if I used my own natural sense of humor. In the three weeks we played at the Ash Grove, I came a long way toward developing a style of performing, although I have never really gotten it all together in the way that Frank must have visualized it. At the end of the Ash Grove engagement, I turned down a tour of the West Coast with folk-blues singer Barbara Dane to go back to New York and sing with John and Scott. John in turn rejected a plea from a childhood friend to go to Spain and become a beach bum!

John Phillips moved into my apartment on West 106 Street, and he and I and Scott rehearsed eight hours or more every day for six weeks, trying to develop enough material for a record. We went through the Schwann record catalog and selected nine record companies to call for an audition. We also called Decca Records, because John and Scott were still under obligation to them through the Smoothies' contract. Of the nine companies we called, all requested sample tapes, except MGM, which agreed to see us live. They offered us a recording contract, but negotiations dragged on as they looked for a hit single for us to record. They felt that our style was good, but they didn't think we had any hit singles in our repertoire. Decca auditioned us, and true to John's guess, they turned us down. The staff producer who heard us was Milt Gabler, a noted jazz buff who hated banjos.

In the midst of our dealings with MGM, we acquired a booking agency, International Talent Associates, or ITA, and a manager, Rene Cardenas, then a partner of Frank Werber, manager of the Kingston Trio. Before we knew it, we were recording for Capitol, the same label that the Kingston Trio recorded on. We went into Capitol's New York studios, hired a bass player named Arnold Fishkin, and recorded our first LP. For the first time, I got to play banjo and guitar on some of the same songs, playing one part and then listening to it with headphones while recording the new part. There was a certain amount of freshness in the blend of Scott's high tenor, John's funkier baritone, and my instrumental abilities. We had to wait six months or so for the record to come out, and in the meantime we played our first live dates at folk clubs in New York and Philadelphia and on a Canadian TV show.

It is hard to explain how I felt about our group, which one of our agents had named the Journeymen. On one level it was sheer pop fluff, but I took pride in playing as well as I could and in learning a bit about group singing from John Phillips, who was an excellent though untrained vocal arranger. Both John and I were writing songs, but his were much more carefully put together, and I felt that I could learn quite a bit about songwriting from him. John benefited by picking up a number of guitar styles from me at our practice and jam sessions. After only four months, we picked up a booking at the Hungry I in San Francisco. It paid $1,500 a week. By the time we got through paying commissions to our agent and manager, it came to about $1,000, but we were convinced that we were on our way.

The Journeymen lasted for three and a half years. In that time we bought out of our management contract while we were almost literally starving, moved out to San Francisco and back to New York, got another manager, and did three LPs for Capitol and a half dozen singles. None of our records really caught on, although they did respectably. We were a musical improvement on the Kingston Trio, because we sang better and played better than they did, but for the most part our hearts weren't in it. We did good shows, and people liked us, but we didn't have the special spark that a Peter, Paul, and Mary seemed to communicate. The last year together was painful. We all had other plans, but we tried to hold the act together, doing concerts and radio commercials for Schlitz Beer. Before the group broke up, Capitol decided to record me as a solo singer. Bob Dylan was just becoming popular, and apparently I was the only one on their label who seemed strange enough to record something similar. I put together an album of "protest songs," mostly topical songs I had written about various matters. The album was called *The Things That Trouble My Mind,* and it is not one of my favorite efforts. I still enjoy some of the songs I wrote for the album, but I never have developed much of an appetite for my singing.

About the time the Journeymen folded our tent and rode into the sunset, a friend of John's named George Wilkins tried to put together a large folk group to play at the 1965 New York World's Fair for 7-Up. John put together a group that included himself, me, Judy Collins, Harry Tuft, rock performer and producer-to-be Felix Pappalardi, and a couple of studio singers. George Wilkins worked for a music house that wrote and produced commercials, and they had dreams of creating a super group that would play Las Vegas lounges, make hit records, and record 7-Up commercials. There were intensive rehearsals, a recording session, and lots of talk followed by lots of silence. At one point we were told that we might be playing at the fair with two English gentlemen, one of whom was supposedly descended from royalty. We thought that this was some sort of joke, but later we discovered that the two English gentlemen were Chad and Jeremy. They became very successful pop-rock stars in the United States and England.

In 1964 I rented an apartment in New York, and a few months later I got married. Toward the end of my Journeymen days, I had gotten very serious about writing songs, and I had more than fifty songs written. I was convinced that songwriting would lead me to fame and fortune, but I was wrong. Over the next few years I was under contract to two different (and respectable) music publishers. I received some reasonably good cash advances, and a number of my songs were recorded on successful albums. I have never been able to make a living by writing songs as a full-time occupation, and I have never written a hit song. My most successful song, "Someone to Talk My Troubles To," was recorded by a dozen different artists, but there were many songs that never got recorded at all.

My financial status improved in 1964 and 1965. I did quite a bit of studio work as an instrumentalist. The folk boom was ending, but the record companies and advertising agencies weren't aware of it. As the popularity of the Beatles spread, I began to see a lot of my studio work dry up. I met a record producer named Dave Edelman while doing some studio work for a company called Cameo Parkway. Dave was producing a "folk" album with Merv Griffin, and he asked me whether I'd like to co-produce it with him. I didn't know what that meant, but I agreed to do it. Through Dave, I met a brilliant engineer named Bill Schwartau, who took me under his wing and showed me how to use the recording studio as a creative tool. Bill was absolutely fearless and adventurous, always willing to try for a special effect or new sound. We became close friends, and my wife and I used to go to his house in Greenwich Village to talk about music and other things. Through my manager, Stan Greeson, I got the chance to produce an album featuring the Kentucky folk singer Jean Ritchie for Warner Brothers. I worked on that project with Bill, and it was thoroughly enjoyable although not commercially successful. Bill and I did some other projects, some of which we sold and many of which we couldn't. One project was a folk-pop recording of studio singers. Bill insisted that I write the vocal parts. At that time I had no idea how to do that, and I ended up enlisting my friend Dan Fox to write the parts, although Bill and the singers thought that I had written the arrangements. Bill simply did not believe that I couldn't write vocal arrangements.

After some unsuccessful experiments producing rock records with a children's radio personality named Beachcomber Bill and the actor Brandon De Wilde, I got the chance to produce some rock singles for Capitol with two different groups, Lothar and the Hand People and The Lost. None of the records became hits, but I learned a great deal about how to make contemporary records and how to budget time, money, and energy in the studio. In 1968, Joe Carlton of ABC Command-Probe Records hired me to work half-time as a record producer for that label. I didn't want to work full-time, because I was making a fair amount of money doing studio work and didn't want to give up playing. The first week I was supposed to start working, the Musicians' Union struck the TV networks and picketed the ABC building. As a member of the union, I was forbidden to cross the line, even though there was no strike against the record company. Fortunately the strike only lasted about a week, and so I was able to start work without much delay.

My first recording project for Command/Probe was to produce an LP by the Glenn Miller band, an orchestra that continues on, although the founder died in World War II. I had never even played on a big band record at that time, let alone been in charge of the session, and I didn't have the faintest idea what I was supposed to do. I found out soon enough that I was supposed to follow the score with a musical road map called a lead sheet. I had to tell the engineer who had the melody parts or what parts of the arrangement were of particular importance. The arranger participated in decisions on how the various musical sections should be balanced, and he instructed some musicians to play louder or softer. It was a rough week for me, but with the help of another producer named John Turner and the engineer, I managed to stagger through it. By the time it was over, I felt that I could produce recordings of different styles and instrumentation.

I suppose that 1968–70 were the peak years of my professional life as a musician in terms of income, work load, and reputation in the music industry. I produced LPs by Dick Hyman, the fine jazz pianist and electronic music composer and player, Doc Severinsen, rock groups, country and western-oriented groups, and a rhythm and blues group. I didn't enjoy recording Severinsen or the Ray Charles singers because the music struck me as being too bland. I really hit my stride with Frummox, a folk-country-rock group, and with Mitchell Braithwaite, a rhythm and blues singer with a light and airy voice that reminded me of Sam Cooke. Frummox was a duo, Steve Fromholz and Dan McCrimmon, who sent me a tape from Denver, where they were working and living. I signed them to ABC-Probe, and they arrived at my house in New Jersey the weekend before the recording sessions. We spent the whole weekend rehearsing songs and arrangements and then went into the recording studio. I did quite a bit of playing on the Frummox album, which is something I usually try to avoid when producing a record. I also hired Eric Weissberg and a fine bassist named John Beal to fill out the band. Steve and Dan brought their friend Travis Holland with them to play extra guitar and mandolin parts.

When a recording session is working well, it is a wonderful experience; it seems that all of modern technology is working with the artist and the musicians to create an entity greater than the sum of its parts. The album was fun to rehearse and exciting to record, and there was a minimum of time-wasting disputes about vocal or instrumental parts. It received favorable critical recognition and sold reasonably well in the group's home terrain of Colorado and Texas. Unfortunately, the record company fell apart in 1969, and the Frummox record became a collector's item, which it remains today, selling for as much as $25 to $35. We put out a single, but it was removed from the play lists of several key radio stations when some listeners protested the use of the word "damn."

Mitchell Braithwaite was a fine singer who wandered into my office one day while he was on a lunch break from pushing carts in the New York garment district. He had a demo record, which I thought sounded really good. I signed him to our label and proceeded to look for the right songs for him to record, since he didn't write songs himself. I went through hundreds of songs before selecting three of them. He and I rehearsed for a number of weeks with me playing rhythm guitar, and then I brought in Bob James to write the arrangements. When we arrived at the recording studio, Mitchell was stunned. He thought that Bob and I would constitute the band, but instead he saw nine pieces, including some horns, and three background singers. After Mitchell recovered from his shock, he did a fine job of singing, even making up some of the harmony on his own. I can remember Jerome Richardson, an excellent saxophone player, listening to the New York Mets baseball game with a transistor radio plugged into one ear while he played. I never figured out how he did that, but it didn't seem to hurt his playing.

Mitchell's record was released twice. The first time it came out, it was totally unsuccessful, but then my boss, Joe Carlton, hired a black promotion man named Jimmy Shaw. Jimmy came into my office dressed in a purple suit and cast a somewhat suspicious eye on me, dressed in corduroys and flannel shirt. I played him a couple of the records I had produced, and then he asked me whether I ever did any rhythm and blues. I played him Mitchell's record, and I thought that he would fall out of the window of my eleventh-floor office. "You did that?" he asked. "That's a hit." I grinned at him and said that I thought so, too. He raced into

Joe Carlton's office and demanded that the recorded be rereleased. It was, and it sold a bit in the southern United States, although it never became a hit. I have no idea where Mitchell Braithwaite is today.

I produced a group called Fat City from Washington, D.C. They were a duo, Bill Danoff and Taffy Nivert, who sang and wrote songs in a sort of folk rock style. They had recorded an excellent demonstration record in a studio in Washington, D.C., and in retrospect I think their demo actually was better than the album we recorded in New York. I wrote a song they recorded called "Wall Street." The song was about an all-night party I had attended in Wall Street, a small town near Boulder, Colorado, in Four Mile Canyon. Although their album didn't do very well, Bill and Taffy hit it big a few years later when they wrote "Take Me Home, Country Roads," with some help from John Denver. They then wrote a song recorded by Denver and by Mary Travers, of Peter, Paul, and Mary. It was called "I Guess He'd Rather Be in Colorado," and it is a description of me and my life as a record producer in New York. This song startled and flattered me, but I was more surprised a few years later to hear Merle Haggard sing it on the television series *Centennial* during the closing segment of the show. It is a bit strange to hear about your life on network television in the context of wholly unrelated events.

I became very dissatisfied with my guitar playing and musicianship, and so I took two years of guitar lessons from Barry Galbraith. Barry is a marvelous jazz player and a very thoughtful person. His independence and integrity are legendary on the New York studio scene, where many musicians would trade their wives or children for employment possibilities. Barry also earned my undying admiration because he was fired from the Kate Smith radio show for not smiling enough. A number of years later he played on a record for Smith with a number of the people who had been in the band for the radio show. The producer of the record knew why Barry had been fired. After the first taping of the first song, he said over the studio inter-com, "That was a pretty good take, you guys, but Barry, could you put more of a smile in your playing?" Of course, everyone in the studio broke up. No one knew whether Kate Smith remembered that incident.

Another facet of Barry's character is that he was the only studio musician I knew who wore flannel shirts to recording sessions during the 1950s. Everyone else wore ties and jackets, but Barry obviously cared more about comfort and sanity than his image. In the early 1960s he was the staff guitarist for the David Frost show, earning over $500 a week. He quit that job, probably the highest-paying steady job in New York, because it was boring to sit there for hours and play nothing or some elementary rhythm pattern.

Working with Barry contributed a good deal to my musical and personal development. It also made me question whether much of the recording work I had done had any relevance to music in general and to my specific musical interests.

Except for one salesman with twenty-four years of seniority, everyone who worked for ABC/Command/Probe Records was fired in 1969. I continued to do studio work as a musician and produced a few records independently without being able to sell them. During the next two years, I went through a painful process of self-evaluation, thinking very seriously about what I had done and what I wanted to do. A number of record companies closed their New York offices and moved to Los Angeles, and I found that I was spending most of my working life playing on commercials. At the age of thirty-five, I could not imagine doing this as a full-time occupation. I wasn't playing or practicing the banjo much, and although I enjoy playing the guitar, my most creative work seems to be done on the banjo. In spring 1971, I went to a club to hear a fine jazz guitarist named Bucky Pizzarelli. He invited me to play a few tunes on the banjo. After I got through, he told me that he had no idea that I played in the particular style I was using in the club. I realized that I had known this man for ten years, had probably played with him on thirty or forty recording sessions, and yet he had no idea of how I really played.

The year before I left New York, 1970, I became involved in

writing and playing music for a show about Frank and Jesse James. The show went through three versions, playing twice at the Bucks County Playhouse in New Hope and later at the Bouwerie Lane Theatre in New York. The actors lived in a big house in New Hope and had a sort of communal theater company. I commuted from my house in New Jersey to work with them. By the time the second version of the show evolved, I had written a half dozen songs for the play, including some of the best things I have ever done. I found it very rewarding to be able to write a song and hear the actors work it into a scene a day or two later.

The show had originated when Jim Keach, Bump Heeter, and Chris Allport were all students in the theater department at Northwestern University. Keach was the younger brother of the actor Stacy Keach, and he tried to use his theatrical contacts to push the show. In summer 1972, I came back to New York from Denver to work on the third version of the show. This version had some good actors and a pretty fair small band, with my friend Ron Lockhart serving as the musical director. Stacy Keach came to visit the show and brought his friend Judy Collins. She decided to invest some money into reworking the show. Chris Allport and John Guth, the other songwriters, dropped out of the work, and I spent the rest of the summer writing more songs.

It was a great time. Stacy, Jim, a writer named Barry Bernstein, and I would brainstorm scenes and ideas for hours, and I would go to sleep and wake up with a song that had seemingly written itself. This is the only time I have ever had this sort of experience. However, we could not find anyone to produce the show. About six years later, the play surfaced as a movie, *The Long Riders,* starring Jim and Stacy Keach and the Carradine brothers. None of the original writers or composers were involved in the movie except for Jim Keach. This resulted in a long and complicated lawsuit that was recently settled out of court. Nevertheless, the Jesse James experience was very positive for me. I enjoyed writing theater music, met some interesting people, and wrote some good songs.

In winter 1971, I got a call from Elliot Lawrence, a composer and arranger, asking whether I'd like to play in a show that was headed for Broadway called *Prettybelle*. This meant some rehearsals in New York and a six-week tryout in Boston, followed by an indefinite stay on Broadway. I went to a reading rehearsal of the show, written by Jule Styne and Robert Merrill, and thought that it was the worst thing I had heard. This didn't faze me; I figured that I knew nothing about Broadway shows, and all the people involved in the show were skilled professionals. Angela Lansbury was the star, and the director was Gower Champion. Howie Collins, an excellent guitarist and part-time cynic, was to be the other guitarist in the show, and he shared my opinion, but how many hit shows had either of us written? A New York rhythm section went up and did the show in January 1971, and the balance of the band were musicians from Boston who often played in shows there. The music was a curious melange of thoroughly arranged bandcharts and relatively loose banjo improvisations. The harmonica player was Richard Hayman, who does many musical arrangements for the Boston Pops Orchestra.

The show had a very confusing effect on me. I was improvising some fairly strange mountain-influenced banjo tunes, but I was also playing rather typical Broadway band charts. There was one rhumba that I never did play quite correctly; the band would wait to see just how I was going to play the part on any given night. I don't know why I didn't get Howie to show me how to play the part correctly, but I didn't.

After a few weeks of performances, it was clear that the show was in trouble. Someone was brought in to doctor the book, and new numbers were hastily thrown in, rearranged, and often thrown out of the show. The inevitable happened. It was announced that the show would close in Boston. The sets were burned, along with a half million dollars of the investors' money. I suppose that I learned several lessons from my work in *Prettybelle*: to trust my initial impressions, which are often correct; never to be an actor, since I could not believe how much more money the musicians were paid for rehearsals and for playing out of town than most of the actors in the play received; and finally to get my musical act together and learn how to read rhythms so that my playing abilities and my responses to musical notation would be in closer alignment.

I decided to leave New York and move to Denver in 1972. I wanted to study music in college and to get out of the eastern United States. I knew that I could get some work in Denver, because my friend Harry Tuft had offered me a chance to teach at the Denver Folklore Center. He was very well established in Denver, and I figured that there would be opportunities in Denver to play or record. I enrolled in the music program at the University of Colorado at Denver to study music arranging and music in general. The decision to leave lifted a gray cloud that had been hanging over my head for a long time. Some of my friends thought that I was crazy to leave New York and its many economic opportunities; others confessed that they too would like to leave. It was a serious decision for me, because it meant uprooting my wife and two-year-old son and going to a place where I had no financial security and would need to lead a simpler life. Although studio work can be quite challenging from a technical point of view it is ultimately frustrating because a musician seldom gets to play what he likes to play or thinks is musically valid. A studio musician is a hired hand, even if the pay is good and the hours are relatively short. The pressure to avoid making mistakes and to express what passes for creativity in the world of recording tends to turn the players into nervous and cynical human beings. The same things that had constrained my music had begun to affect my personal relationships, and this made leaving easier. It was clear that if I stayed around New York, I would not remain married.

I spent the next two years getting a B.A. in music, studying the usual round of sight-singing and harmony, music history, and theory. I spent a good deal of time reacquainting myself with the banjo and feeling good about playing music. Music jobs in Colorado pay very poorly in comparison with New York, but I gradually realized that I could gain some musical flexibility in compensation for the loss of income. In New York, the people who hired me to play guitar seldom used me to play banjo, and vice versa. In Colorado, I got the opportunity to write film scores, played all sorts of club dates, and even performed some of my own music in public for the first time in years.

I found the first year of school very difficult, because I had little patience with some of the elementary things I was studying or with my own inability to learn the technical aspects of music as quickly as I wished. As I neared the end of my college career, I got the opportunity to teach about the music industry in a new program at Colorado Women's College. CWC was one of thirty-five or forty schools that included the music industry in their music programs. I taught there for six years before being fired along with three-fourths of the faculty in a series of disputes with the college's administration. Teaching other people about the music business helped me clarify where I fit into the world of music and where I chose not to do so. It was a good experience for me, and I felt that I contributed some useful information to students who generally had little practical experience in dealing with the music industry.

Around 1973, my friend and part-time musical guru Dan Fox suggested that I write a method book for a five-string banjo. I drew heavily on his experiences as a composer, arranger, and music editor, and over the next four years I wrote a three-volume method series for the banjo. The books have been quite successful, especially the beginner's guide. This led me into a whole new career as a writer of books about music. In 1976, Harry Tuft decided to write a revised edition of the mail-order catalog he had written some years earlier. A friend of his contacted Alfred Knopf, and they agreed to publish the book, whereupon Harry decided that he did not want to write it. I took on the task with another musician, Larry Sandberg. For two years we researched every available book and record that included North American folk music, and in 1976 we completed *The Folk Music Source-book*. In 1977, the book won the Deems Taylor ASCAP Music Critics Award.

Since I had become a writer, I decided to try another writing project, which culminated in *The Music Business: Career Opportunities and Self-Defense,* published by Crown in 1979 and now in its fourth printing.

In 1976 and 1977, I wrote a thirty-minute score for an educational television show called the *Colorado Bicentennial Folk Ballet.* I wrote the music for a number of instruments, including fiddle, banjo, mandolin, dobro, cello, flute, piano, and percussion. Shortly after I finished this project, I got to write five songs and thirty minutes of instrumental music for a film called *The Edge,* which is about sports that involve the risk of death, such as hang gliding. In both of these projects, Harry Tuft served as a musical director and adviser. I needed every bit of his advice, even when I didn't take it.

In thinking about the future, I find myself looking at my experiences and the careers of my friends and musical associates. My future plans have turned increasingly to writing and to performing and composing music as an auxiliary career. I would just as soon play only the music that I want to play and avoid audiences that are not interested in hearing something new. I am not essentially a performer but am more interested in writing and recording music. I still play occasional commerical music jobs, but my inclination is to phase out this area of music, because I don't enjoy it and don't need the money. Harry Tuft and I have put together a program about life and music in the western United States and have presented it in several locations in Colorado. We have done a fair amount of research for this project, which includes traditional songs, cowboy songs from the movies of the 1930s and 1940s, and some contemporary songs. We hope to make a record of this program and perform it in other parts of the country. For 1981–82, I have a National Endowment for the Humanities grant to write a book about a black musician named Wesley Westbrooks who lives in Denver. Wesley writes gospel music but has been cleaning airplanes for a living for twenty-four years. I do not know whether I will return to college teaching. I still perform music, most recently at the Winnipeg Folk Festival in Canada, and I have an LP of banjo music, mostly instrumental music that I have written.

Most of the musicians I know who are unhappy do not have clear goals. They are not sure whether they want commercial success or whether their primary goal is to communicate some sort of individual style of music to an audience. It is easy to say that both objectives are possible; however, this is not usually the case. I think that a brief career aimed at making it in the popular music field is instructive for a young musician, provided that the impetus to succeed does not overwhelm the desire to create or perform the music that a musician wants to play. In my own life there were too many times in New York when I found myself on the wrong side of that cliff, looking for a big pay-off while playing music that offended me.

I would recommend to anyone seeking a career in music that he or she develop as much versatility as possible, not only in music but in the ability to pursue other professions. Most of the Creole jazzmen in New Orleans had trades that can support them in a stable life-style, such as bricklaying or plastering. The problem with being too closely identified with one musical style is that if the style becomes outmoded or unfashionable, it becomes impossible to get work. By wandering through careers as a performing musician, studio player, songwriter, record producer, college teacher, and writer, I have managed to remain employable over the years. I have also found that my life remains interesting, because each career has different challenges and objectives. I personally like the feeling that I never know what I will be doing next. Any aspiring musician needs to consider what can be done if the career he or she covets becomes unavailable or impractical. As Pete Seeger says in *The Incomplete Folksinger*, people should learn the value of improvisation in life. If one road is impassable, try another one, even if you have to build it yourself.

THE LIFE AND MUSIC OF
THE AMERICAN COWBOY

The life of the cowboy has fascinated Americans since the late nineteenth century. This interest is evidenced by the massive outpouring of films, records, songs, television shows, and rodeo performances throughout North America. The music of the cowboy spans three styles of music and is marked by powerful cultural changes in American society. Traditional cowboy songs were collected by folklorists, the music of the Hollywood cowboys was written for motion pictures, and the current crop of songs about cowboys generally represents music composed by contemporary folk and country singers from the viewpoint of the singer-songwriter. In these recent songs, the writer generally keeps one eye glued to the country and popular music record surveys, charting the hits that are the calling card of success in popular music. In this survey I will discuss all these idioms and historical periods, with a short look at the music of the Hollywood cowboy and some speculations about the lost or largely unreported music of the black cowboy. I will touch upon the music of the Mexican cowboy in passing.

The collectors of cowboy music started their work in the 1890s. The first serious western folklorist was Cowboy Jack Tharp, who was a professional cowboy. In 1889–90 he took a lengthy horseback trip through a half dozen southwestern states. He played the banjo-mandolin, a portable instrument that could be stuffed in a large saddlebag. By memorizing the songs that he collected and playing them back to his informants, Tharp was able to learn songs without the aid of a tape recorder or the ability to notate music. Clark Stanley published the first, if fragmentary, collection in 1897,[1] Tharp published his own work in 1908,[2] and John Lomax, the famous collector of American folk songs, jumped into the fray with his collection of cowboy songs in 1910.[3]

Lomax's collection was the first to achieve broad distribution, and he reprinted several songs that Tharp had composed. Lomax was probably unaware of this at the time, because Tharp did not credit himself with authorship in the original edition of his book. Tharp had no particular love for Lomax, referring to him sarcastically as "the learned professor" in a subsequent edition of his own book. Lomax habitually edited and also expurgated many of his printed texts, often combining several variants into a single version. Lomax was a professor of English, and he probably thought it advisable to make editorial improvements in the texts. In other instances he was undoubtedly laundering bawdy material. Because Lomax had compiled the texts and since they had not existed in the specific versions in which he published them, he could assert copyright claims to many of the songs. Later on, I will discuss Lomax's techniques of collecting songs and also some of the limitations of his method.

The traditional cowboy songs found in the collections and cited above usually describe the life of the cowboy on the ranch, riding on the trail, or in the world of fantasy. The focus is on horses, love, reminiscence and nostalgia, outlaws, Indians, tragedies, paradise on earth, the working life of the cowboy, heroes and heroic deeds, and religion and death. These were the songs that passed into oral tradition in the late nineteenth century and the early part of the twentieth century.

The various song types favor certain themes. They repeatedly have the same subject. First of all, there is the horse, the cowboy's constant companion. Two kinds of horses found their way into cowboy songs. One was the cowboy's friend, companion, and co-worker. This sort of horse, like the White Steed of the Prairies or Pattonio, the Pride of the Plains, was a faithful and heroic creature. The other was a bronco, or outlaw horse, that provided a test of the hero's manhood and courage. Sometimes only the hero could ride such a horse, as in the song "To Midnight." Occasionally an outlaw horse would be used to play a joke on a tenderfoot, or novice cowboy, as in "The Zebra Dun." In this instance, the greenhorn turns out to be an expert rider. He masters the beast, and all the cowboys have a good laugh at themselves.

The image of women in cowboy songs represents the classic nineteenth-century dichotomy between the good woman and the evil temptress. The wife-mother-sister-sweetheart is placed on a pedestal. She is beautiful, inaccessible, and demanding. The dance-hall girl is available for a price, rough and tough. In the many ballads that memorialize dying cowboys, the hero usually expresses deep concern about the "good" woman. The Dying Ranger, in the song of that title, begs his comrades to take care of his wife and sister, and they agree to do so.

Sometimes the wonderful woman turns out to be a tramp. In "The Girl I Left Behind," the cowboy loses his sweetheart when he goes on a long cattle drive. In the classic ballad "Trail to Mexico," the girl begs her cowboy sweetheart not to go off on such a drive. When he does, she leaves him for another, wealthier man. Several writers report songs that use blatant sexual images, such as boasts of phallic size, or songs about sodomy or venereal disease, but it is difficult to find printed texts that bear out these reports.[4] J. Frank Dobie, the Texas folklorist, describes campfire contests in which cowboys attempted to outdo one another in singing bawdy songs.[5]

The end of the cowboy era was mourned by songs of reminiscence and nostalgia. In some songs the cowboy recalled his youth, and in others he described a specific event, such as a Christmas ball. Some of the nostalgic songs had touches of bitterness directed against farmers, sheepherders, civilization as the enemy of a natural life, and the irreversible ravages of old age. The theme of the cowboy as an extinct or endangered species is explored in such songs as "The Old Scout's Lament" and "The Lone Buffalo Hunters."[6]

Cattle stampedes were the inspiration for many songs about death or serious injury. These tragedies were caused by bulls, wild horses, outlaws, Indian attacks, or combinations of these events. Occasionally the tragedy resulted from an act of nature, as in "Cyclone Blues."

Many songs lament the hardships of life on the range, but others describe cowboy life as paradise on earth. The hero of "A Kansas Cowboy" complains about the hard work a cowboy must do but then exclaims that he'd rather be a cowboy than anything else in the world. "The Cowboy's Life" simply extols the delights of being a cowboy.

Work songs describe working conditions or complain about them. Descriptive songs deal with rustlers, stampedes, branding cows, or riding wild horses. The songs of complaint tend to be about natural disasters, stampedes, rustlers, Indians, injuries, nesters, poverty, or generally hard work. A few verses in "The Old Chisholm Trail" accuse the boss of cheating, and there is an epic ballad, "The Buffalo Skinners," in which the men on a trail drive kill the boss when he refuses to pay them; but for the most part, few songs manifest the sort of class consciousness that is so common in mining songs. In the cowboy era, many bosses worked alongside the cowhands so that there may have been only little resentment against the ranch owners. This changed as cattle raising became a big business, but by that time most of the traditional songs were well established, and the cowboys of the silver screen did not worry about class consciousness.

There are no cowboy heroes of truly mythic dimensions, such as Paul Bunyan, the legendary lumberjack, or John Henry, the steel-driving man. Pecos Bill was a legendary cowboy, tough as nails. He played with rattlesnakes and wrestled bears, but he was more like Mike Fink, the riverboat hero, than a superman. The heroes who do turn up in cowboy songs, such as Little Joe, the Wrangler, or Bill Peters, the stagecoach driver, usually die in the performance of their heroic deeds rather than run off to perform a series of incredible feats. In several songs, such as "Utah Carroll," the cowboy dies while rescuing the boss's daughter from a stampeding herd. In some of the more recent songs, such as "Pete Knight,"[7] the hero is killed while trying to ride a wild horse.

Cowboy humor is often directed at the cowboy himself. He delights in creating embarrassing situations for a tenderfoot, but in "The Zebra Dun," the cowboy has to admit that "every educated fellow ain't a plumb greenhorn." Occasionally cowboys would put each other on by dressing as greenhorns and then riding the roughest bronc in the corral. Another sort of humor was to make fun of a particular group or region. The song, "Texas Girls" says that "You can give marriage a whirl, if you've got some cash in your purse, but don't marry no one but a Texas girl, 'cause no matter what's happened they've seen worse."[8] Other songs made fun of such groups as Kansans, Arizonans, and egotistical cowboys.

Austin and Alta Fife point out that some cowboy songs about religion used old hymm tunes, while others parodied cowboy songs, using religious words with familiar secular tunes.[9] In the song "Silver Jack," a doubting cowboy is forced to acknowledge Christ by a group of cowboys who beat him up. In "The Cowman's Prayer," the singer asks God to bless his cattle. The singer of "The Cowboy's Meditation" wonders whether people live on stars and whether he will see his mother again in heaven.[10]

The outlaws Sam Bass and Jesse James appear in Robin Hood roles. In both groups of songs, the outlaw is betrayed by a traitorous member of the gang. The heroes of "The Wild Rattling Cowboy" and "The Dying Desperado" get into trouble because they take revenge on hombres who have fooled around with their sweethearts. Occasionally an outlaw is an unregenerate hard case, like Billy the Kid or Quantrell. These ruffians have little to recommend them, even in song. The Jesse James story and song seem to be familiar to almost everyone in the United States. Every year there are new movies, plays, and songs about Jesse and Frank, such as the recent movie *The Long Riders*. The alleged Robin Hood qualities of Frank and Jesse, who "stole from the rich and gave to the poor," seem to have captured the national imagination. Most Americans are familiar with Jesse's betrayal by Robert Ford, the dirty little coward, who was hired to infiltrate the gang and kill Jesse. Robert did so, aided by his brother Charley; they shot Jesse in the back while he was adjusting a picture in his own home.

Miscellaneous songs encountered in collections of cowboy music cover such subjects as tributes to the Texas Rangers, drinking, home and mother, hell, desperadoes, and Indians. A few cowboy songs, such as "Sioux Indians" or "The Buffalo Skinners," are epic ballads, telling complete stories in song.

Any classificatory scheme has its limits, and it is evident that many of these songs cover several subjects. "The Buffalo Skinners" tells of the perils of the trail drive and is also a complaint against mean bosses and miserable working conditions. Songs of reminiscence may also detail memories of a loved horse, tragedies are intertwined with love stories, and some songs cover a wide variety of subjects.

Lomax's book of cowboy songs was a major influence on the music itself. The book was reprinted and revised a number of times and is still available. During the 1920s and 1930s, a number of singing cowboys made recordings and had their own radio shows. Carl Sprague's recording "When the Work's All Done This Fall" sold 900,000 copies. During the middle and late 1920s, record companies became aware that there was a market for cowboy songs among people who were not interested in classical music or show tunes. Jimmie Rodgers and Carson Robison were popular artists who recorded some cowboy songs. Gene Autry was a successful recording artist even before the start of his motion picture career. Radio artists Powder River Jack and Kitty Lee, George German, and John White all were "singing cowboys" with their own radio programs.

The influence of the cowboy in the various media reached its height in the 1930s and 1940s. The image of the cowboy that originated in the nineteenth century as a sort of vagrant and drifter, the scourge of the Kansas cow towns, changed to one of nobility and courage. The cowboy was still a tough hombre, but only if you crossed him. Usually he was a faithful and good friend, loyal to his horse, woman, God, and country. More than any other single individual, William (Buffalo Bill) Cody brought about this change. Cody was not a cowboy but a buffalo hunter and trail guide who started a Wild West show featuring Buck Taylor. Bill also persuaded the publishers of the Dime Library to immortalize Buck in their pulp novels. Cody's Wild West Show and the shows of his competitors, such as the Miller Brothers 101 Ranch Show featuring the black bull roper Bill Pickett, toured the major cities of the United States and Europe. These shows featured fake gunfights, roping and marksmanship exhibitions, and lots of trick riding.

The image of the cowboy that many people hold today was born in these performances. The cowboy was the last individual guardian of the American frontier. He shared the wilderness with animals and Indians. He was a hero-vigilante, making sure that the law was honored and respected by all. The radio and television hero the Lone Ranger was a paradigm for this sort of hero. He was totally ethical, yet he wore a mask and operated outside the law. In most episodes he was suspected of being a criminal and had to prove himself a man of honor. The whole concept seems to convey a distrust of our system of law and order. The orthodox lawmen seem ill equipped to handle the vicious outlaws; only this anti-hero with his "faithful Indian companion" can bring the evil villains to their knees.

The movies brought the cowboy to new heights of popularity. Silent movies featured such cowboy heroes as William Hart and Tom Mix. After the talkies arrived, the cowboys began to sing on screen. In the middle of the action, Gene Autry, Eddie Dean, or Jimmy Wakely would break into song, strumming a guitar as a big band played in the background. Of course, traditional cowboy songs were often sung without instrumental accompaniment. The most popular instruments on the working ranch were the fiddle and then the banjo. The guitar was comparatively rare. Movie cowboys always played the guitar. The songs that were sung in the movies were self-conscious attempts at pop music hits, featuring what are called "hooks" in the music business. A hook is a recurring lyric or musical phrase that is designed to get the listener involved with a song. Often the hook is also the title of the song, as in Gene Autry's "Back in the Saddle Again." Traditional cowboy songs such as "The Streets of Laredo" usually had a single melodic theme that was repeated throughout the song. The songs of the movie cowboys had two parts, including a verse and a recurring chorus. Sometimes they even contained a third part, or musical bridge, designed to provide melodic contrast. These concepts remain the foundation for modern cowboy songwriting. A hit song could help the sale of movie tickets, which in turn contributed to record sales. Gene Autry and Tex Ritter recorded quite a few hits, and Autry, and later Roy Rogers, endorsed guitars, clothers, and miscellaneous items in the merchandizing process familiar to us today through such media smashes as *Star Wars*.

Although the movies expanded the popularity of the cowboy, they also helped bring about the end of traditional cowboy songs. Today, country music stars will sing an occasional obligatory cowboy song like "Little Joe the Wrangler," but traditional cowboy songs constitute a very small portion of the country and western repertoire. Radio cowboys disappeared with the domination of the movies and television, and by 1940 the radio cowboy had ridden his last range. A number of the hit songs of the movie cowboys were written by Bob Nolan, of the Sons of the Pioneers. Some of these songs, such as "Cool Water" and "Tumbling Tumbleweeds," remain popular today.

The rise of television after the end of World War II introduced new cowboy heroes and revived the career of the old movie star Hopalong Cassidy. Gene Autry even produced a television series about Annie Oakley. In the 1950s and 1960s, such staples of television as *Gunsmoke*, *The Virginian*, *Rawhide*, and *Bonanza* arrived. These shows featured more violence than the cowboy movie epics of the 1940s. They also used actors who did not sing or play the guitar. Music was relegated to the title song and background scoring. There was no more singing on horseback and no more interruption of a script to fit a song into the story. Occasionally a guest star would be a drifter-singer passing through a town or ranch who might do some performing. One regular character on *The Virginian* occasionally played guitar and sang.

By the time John Wayne and Clint Eastwood became the leading cowboys of the screen, the era of the singing cowboy had come to an end. The urban folk music revival of the middle 1950s and early 1960s brought about a new interest in traditional cowboy music. Local folk song societies formed in many states, some of which promoted concerts and even issued recordings of traditional singers. Glenn Ohrlin, a cowboy and something of a folk song collector and scholar, recorded several albums for local folk song societies and later for the Philo Record Company. He subsequently put together a collection of cowboy songs published by the University of Illinois Press.[11] Gail Gardner, a cowboy, a poet, and a graduate of Dartmouth College, published a collection of his lyrics and also did some recording for the Arizona Friends of Folk Music.[12] His friend Billy Simon wrote melodies for some of Gail's lyrics. Oak Publications reissued Margaret Larkin's collection of cowboy songs in 1963,[13] and the Fifes, folk song scholars from Utah, reprinted Tharp's original collection along with tunes for his lyrics and additional versions and carefully researched histories of the songs.[14]

There appeared to be a considerable and sincere interest in authentic cowboy songs; however, a curious fact has since emerged. A large number of cowboy songs were traceable to specific composers and lyricists. To most collectors, these songs qualified as folk songs because they had appeared in the oral tradition, passed along from one cowboy to another. In other areas of American folk music, we are aware of the existence of such folk composers as Larry Gorman, the Maine lumberjack, and Aunt Molly Jackson, the mining bard from Harlan County, Kentucky, but there is no other area of American folk music where so many songs can be traced to specific composers and lyricists. Through the careful scholarship of the Fifes, White, Ohrlin, and others, we know that the composed songs included such favorites as Curley Fletcher's "Strawberry Roan," Harry Stephens's "Night Herding Song," cowboy poet D. J. O'Malley's "Charlie Rutledge" and "When The Work's All Done This Fall," Romaine Lowdermilk's "The Big Corral" and "A Busted Cowboy's Christmas," Larry Chittenden's lyrics for the "Cowboy's Christmas Ball" and "Speckles," Jack Tharp's "The Pecos River Queen," "Whose Old Cow," and "Speckles," James Grafton Rogers's lyrics for "Delores" and "Long Ride on the Santa Fe Trail,"[15] George German's "I Learned about Horses from Him," and Agnes Morley Cleveland's "Charge of the LOC Steer" and "When Bob Got Throwed." Many of the cowboy songwriters and performers, such as Gail Gardner and Carl Sprague, were college graduates, and others, such as Harry Stephens, had attended college.

By the 1970s the folk song revival had come to an end, but some interesting changes were taking place in commercial country and western music. A new breed of songwriters emerged who treated complex subjects in a refreshing way. Mickey Newbury, Kris Kristoffersen, and others shook the Tin Pan Alley–Nashville types by introducing sophisticated subjects and lyrics. By the mid-1970s, several country music stars, including Willie Nelson and Waylon Jennings, began growing their hair and referring to themselves as "the outlaws." They saw themselves as western rather than southern artists, and their dress was closer to earthy styles than to the star-spangled Hollywood-tailored outfits of the older country singers such as Hank Snow or Red Foley. Other singers with a similar orientation but more of a folk music preference, such as Steve Fromholz and Michael Murphy, began to sing and write songs about metaphorical cowboys. The distinctions between this sort of country music and rock and roll began to disappear, and before long insurance salesmen were practicing fast draws in suburban basements while listening to songs like "Desperado," written and recorded by the Eagles, a country-influenced rock group.

The lyric content of the outlaws' song tended to be violent and antisocial, setting the singer up in a gunfighter pose. Society and the media had become more permissive toward violence, and thus the western hero became more violent. Gallantry was on the wane, and sex and violence had become the currency of the day. Sam Peckinpah, director of *The Wild Bunch,* was one of the trend setters of the violent western. *The Long Riders,* a 1980 film about the James gang, portrays the gang as an unpredictable group of neurotics rather than the misunderstood Robin Hoods of earlier movie portraits. The contemporary cowboy as seen by the media today is no longer the lonesome and misunderstood good guy. He is a slightly homicidal bully spoiling for a fight, an unpredictable and untrustworthy character no longer fit to honor a mother, wife, or sister. The mild and friendly hero of yesterday has become the violent loner of today. The good guy has become a bad guy.

Alongside this new stereotype of the cowboy, more sympathetic and sophisticated writer-singers such as Mary McCaslin, Steve Fromholz, Michael Murphy, Utah Phillips, and Ian Tyson have created a different type of character. Fromholz's "The Man with the Big Hat" pays tribute to the cowboy, examining him as a dying breed. When Fromholz's group, Frummox, recorded the song, they enlisted Jerry Jeff Walker to sing along on the choruses. Instead of singing "the man with the big hat is buying," Walker sang that he was "dying," adding another level of interpretation to the song.[16] McCaslin uses the word "west" as a metaphor for freedom in her song "Way Out West."[17] In the land of open spaces and skies, one cannot be tied down in personal relationships, which represent bondage. She presents the cowboy as the last free man. Utah Phillips has written a number of songs about cowboys, some factual and other romantic. One song, "The Goodnight Loving Trail," is about a camp cook, "the old woman."[18]

The folk-influenced image of the cowboy as the last free man is quite different from the country outlaw pose. Although an outlaw may be free in a superficial sense, the end point for most outlaws is jail or death. Of course, to see the cowboy as a free man represents a naive point of view. On a large ranch, the cowboy is a wage slave in much the same sense as a Ford assembly-line worker or an IBM office functionary. Still, there is an abstract sense in which the cowboy probably is one of the last free men. There is something about working in comparative isolation, out of doors, viewing endless prairies, mountains, or skies, that is different from working in a city office building or on a hot assembly line.

The romantic image of the cowboy, when it is not overloaded with gaudy sentimentality, may represent the final and logical musical statement of the value of the cowboy in our society. There is no shortage of books and articles debunking the cowboy legend. The Western scholar William Savage makes quite a plea for more careful research, for examining the reality of the cowboy's life as opposed to the legend.[19] What do we really know about the cowboy's life? How many cowboys were there? How many were black or Mexican, and how many were the descendants of English gentlemen?

There seems to be something unsettling to the modern historian or social scientist in dealing with nonsubstantive material. The cowboy must have been a bit of a jerk, they seem to say. After all, who would want to work far from home for a small amount of money in an uncomfortable environment? Perhaps social scientists have missed the meaning of the cowboy experience. What does it matter, for example, whether John Henry really lived or whether he is a legend of the mind alone? His importance transcends literal reality. He was a man, and he defeated the machine, dying in the struggle.

What the cowboy accomplished was to open the American West for settlement, for ranching and farming. He did it with a sense of humor, taking what was essentially a boring, dirty, and underpaid job and making it into the stuff of myths. No matter that he got help from Buffalo Bill, from Owen Wister in his novel *The Virginian,* from Remington's paintings, and from a dozen stars of stage, screen, and radio. Granted that today the cowboy image is a selling tool for beer, clothes, cigarettes, cereal, and a hundred other products. Could that image of the cowboy be used if it didn't ring a bell or touch a nerve in the hearts of most Americans?

A number of aspects of the cowboy mystique relate to the secret life of many Americans. The cowboy's code was a code of honor. The agreements between people were personal rather than financial. In Jane Kramer's *The Last Cowboy,* the protagonist cannot bring himself to put an agreement with his boss into writing.[20] A man's word should be his guarantee; contracts are for lawyers and bankers. This charming commonsense notion hearkens back to a time and a feeling that for many of us represents the essence of American values, the ability to relate to people based on mutual goals and trust. The cowboy was a man of action, whereas today we live in a computerized world in which it is difficult to get a yes or no answer to a question. When a record company refuses to give an artist a contract, they don't say no, they "pass for now." When a functionary in an office wants to stall some inconsequential request that we are making, he will "get back to us." We live in an era of indecision. Most of us see the cowboy as a man who had his horse, his gun, and a lot of guts. If the cattle stampeded, he didn't ask a bureaucrat what to do. He controlled his own life and accepted the consequences. This ability to act is what we lack and yearn for in an age of bureaucracy.

Other aspects of a working cowboy life are less specifically functional and more abstract, but they are equally significant. Imagine what it was like to be alone in a mountain wilderness area or on an endless prairie. Imagine riding through country that few have seen before, sleeping out under the stars with only a horse and a few friends for companions. Today, everywhere we go, we find noise, litter, and other people. The cowboy had to create his own diversions and entertainments.

Some men probably yearn for the cowboy's freedom from the demands of women. Cowboy society was a male cooperative, and very few women were around. Many men are confused by the modern woman's need for freedom and equality. Such men might prefer an era when women were idols or whores, if they were not simply absent from the scene. All of this ignores the loneliness and frustration of the real-life cowboy. How much fun was a ranch dance where there were ten men for every woman? How attractive was the inevitable sodomy or homosexuality that accompanies the absence of women?

The positive cooperative spirit of the roundup has disappeared as corporate farms have replaced the individualism of the old-time cowboy. Most of the cattle range is fenced, the roads are paved, and four-wheel-drive vehicles take us almost everywhere. Our lives and dreams are indeed fenced in, and we see the cowboy's life as one that surpassed our contemporary limitations, in our eyes a life of freedom and fellowship.

The rodeo and the rodeo cowboy represent a sort of out-of-phase extension of the cowboy dream. The rodeo cowboy is more like a professional athlete than a cowboy, even though quite a few started as working cowboys. The cowboy dream is distorted in the rodeo in that all the energies that go into rodeo are necessarily more competitive than cooperative. The rodeo cowboy competes for money; the real cowboy cooperated because he loved his work and had to work with others to survive. The love of a rodeo cowboy for his work is more like the obsession of a gambler for a deck of cards. The rodeo cowboy's life is like an endless cattle drive, with hundreds of events all over North America. Although the life of the cowboy also has its perils, the rodeo cowboy has to live like a bullfighter. Danger is his constant companion. It is interesting to note that the two television series that dramatized the life of the rodeo cowboy, *Stoney Burke* and *Wide Country,* were not successful. Although Americans are fascinated by rodeo as a competitive sport, the relationship between the rodeo cowboy and the cowboy life myth apparently was not sufficient to sustain these programs.

It was inevitable that the rodeo cowboy would become an entertainer, a modern-day Gene Autry. Thus we have Larry Mahan, Chris Le Doux, Ivan Daines,[21] and others. The songs of the rodeo cowboy are like those of the movie cowboys, contemporary songs aimed at the hit parade. Rodeo cowboy singers tell about loneliness, rodeo clowns who were once competitors, truck stops, travel, accidents, drinking, rough horses, rodeo groupies, victories, and defeats. Some of their songs pay tribute to the old cowboys and the cowboy legend. None of the rodeo singers has achieved anything like the popularity of Gene Autry. Larry Mahan was a real-life rodeo champion before he became a singer, but he achieved more success as a rodeo cowboy than as an entertainer. It may be a matter of talent, but I suspect that it is more a matter of timing. The rodeo simply does not carry the nostalgic appeal that the cowboy legend holds for most Americans.

Some contemporary folk-inspired writer-singers, such as Ian Tyson and Mike Williams, sing songs about rodeo people that are more romantic and less specifically about rodeo experiences than the songs of the rodeo cowboys. Tyson's "Someday Soon" describes the love of a young girl for a rodeo cowboy.[22] She asserts that she will follow him anywhere, even though her parents disapprove. This "appeal of the drifter" theme has appeared in countless pop and blues songs.[23] The appeal of the mysterious stranger to a young girl is a universal theme that is not necessarily tied to the rodeo experience. A rendezvous or life with him promises experiences and entertainments far beyond the confines of a particular town or time. In Alex Bevan's "Rodeo Rider," sung by Lew London, the protagonist is a failed rodeo rider with a college education who is headed for a life riding fence in Montana.[24] In these songs, the rodeo experience merges with the cowboy myth. They are probably as close as songs can be to the

American image of the cowboy experience. This may explain the appeal of Ian Tyson's song, which is also well-written, melodic, coherent, and easy to sing.

There have been some flirtations between the older country singers and cowboy themes. Marty Robbins has had a number of hits with cowboy themes, usually involving gunfighters. "El Paso," "Big Iron," and "Running Gun" are songs about the violent aspects of the cowboy legend. "El Paso" remains a country standard, with its Mexican-flavored guitar style. The theme of the cowboy with the Mexican girl friend is familiar in traditional cowboy music as well as the Nashville version. The subjects of Robbins's western songs are outlaws, guns, running away, and the like. No other country singer has mined this territory so exhaustively, although *Bonanza* star Lorne Greene had something of a hit with his gunfighter song "Ringo."

The music of the traditional cowboy song differs somewhat from that of other American folk songs. There are a remarkable number of songs in 3/4 and 6/8 time, reflecting a strong Irish influence. Many cowboy songs have rather commonplace melodies. This may have been a result of the increased use of the guitar. The banjo and fiddle are less chord-based than the guitar, and they allow for freer interpretation of unusual melodies, particularly the modal melodies found in the southern Appalachian mountains. The guitar has a tendency to homogenize melodies and force them into simple chord progressions. Of course, unaccompanied singing allows the most flexibility, both rhythmically and melodically. Since the increase in popularity of the guitar coincided with the expansion of song-collecting activities, the guitar almost certainly had an effect on the final shape of the melodies of many cowboy songs. Once the movie cowboys appeared with their guitars, many of the dude ranches encouraged cowboys to sing and play guitar so that visitors could recreate the mythical Autry–Rogers experience around the campfire. A really fine guitarist can overcome the limitations of a chord-centered accompaniment instrument, but few cowboys were expert guitar pickers. Another reason for the lack of interesting melodies is that many of the tunes were simply vehicles for remembering poems by such cowboy poets as Charles Badger Clark, Henry Herbert Knibbs, and Gail Gardner. The melodies were not intended as independent creations but as vehicles for memorizing the texts.

One of the puzzles that emerges in an examination of cowboy songs is the limited amount of black influence. If black cowboys represented a sizable proportion of the cowboy population, why weren't more black musical influences present?[25] We might expect to find more 4/4 rhythms, the presence of blue notes, which are the flatted third and seventh notes of the major scale, and blues verse forms with repeated lines and spoken interjections between lines. Lomax's method of collecting songs was to write a thousand letters to newspapers requesting that readers submit songs to him. One wonders whether he wrote to black or Spanish-language newspapers or whether many people could not or did not read his queries. In an article written for the *Journal of American Folklore* in 1915, Lomax asserted that little collecting work had been done among black and Spanish groups in Texas.[26] The few black cowboy songs Lomax did find turned up during his visits to Texas prisons some years after the publication of his original cowboy collection. These included Leadbelly's "When I Was a Cowboy," a strange version of "The Old Chisholm Trail" by Clear Rock Platt, and Iron Head Baker's variant of "Streets of Laredo." Baker's song was a sort of transition version between the "Streets of Laredo" and "St. James Infirmary."[27] The only other reference Lomax makes to black cowboy songs is to attribute "The Zebra Dun" to a black camp cook.[28] The song itself shows no black musical or textual influences.

Looking back on the work of Lomax and Tharp seventy years later, I wonder how many songs of black origin were lost to us because the collectors did not have enough contact with black cowboys. In Teddy Blue Abbott's book *We Pointed Them North*, there is a song called "The Ogalally Song" which the author says was written by a black cowboy around 1881 near Ogalally on the South Platte River.[29] The song was sung by its author, John Henry. It describes the boss, the boss's family, and his partner. This is the one song I have found outside of Lomax's Texas prison songs that is clearly written by a black cowboy. It contains numerous blue notes and spoken interjections of o-o-oh and y-y-ye, and it mentions the singer in the first person, a device typical of blues songs. Blue describes how he himself made up additional verses to the song as the trail drive continued. He prints these verses, which concern other locations along the drive, with the same tune, and then shows how he wrote another set of verses to this tune about a girl named Cowboy Annie in Miles City, Montana.

Another version of the Ogalally song appears in the book *Kansas Folklore*.[30] This version was collected in Dighton, Kansas, in 1954. No tune is printed with the text, but the spoken interjections in the Abbott book are gone, as is any mention of John Henry or his boss, Ab Blocker. The Kansas version tells of crossing the Colorado, Red, and Washita rivers, arriving in Dodge City, and continuing north. I regard this as a white version of a black song, revised to suit the singer and his peers.

Abbott states that another set of lyrics about the Lou'siana Lowlands was also sung to the Ogalally melody.[31] If this melody and two texts could emerge from a single black cowhand, we must ask why similar songs didn't emerge from Lomax's informants, or appear in the collections of other scholars. Perhaps these scholars had only limited contact with black cowboys. We also have little accurate information on the population profile of the black cowboy. Did the number of black cowboys decrease as the intensity of folk song collection increased?

In the museum of the Black American West Foundation in Denver, I found several pictures and paintings of black cowboy-musicians. These included a picture of a black mandolin player from Colorado Springs named W. E. Proctor, who lived from 1900 to 1935, and a painting of a black cowboy playing guitar.[32]

How many such musicians were there? What kind of music did they play?

A number of the older black musicians in the United States have a repertoire that includes white folk songs, such as square dance tunes.[33] Perhaps some of the black cowboys wrote or sang music in a "white" style, as Lomax's notes on "The Zebra Dun" suggest. Although it is too late to remedy the musical neglect of the black cowboy, perhaps some of this music can still be preserved through the help of oral histories, Foxfire-style projects, and recordings and videotapes.

What is the future of the cowboy image in American life? Although the cowboy of the 1980s may well be considered a caricature of the real-life cowboy of the late nineteenth century, there is no question that the image of the cowboy in contemporary American life glorifies the value systems connected with individuality, self-confidence, courage, and loyalty. Although the "urban cowboy" may have a streak of the nonconformist in his makeup, what we admire in the old-time cowboy is the ability he showed to make decisions and then take action. There is every reason to believe that these values will continue to be admired in our society.

THE CONTEMPORARY MUSIC
EDUCATOR

Music education could be a vital and dynamic aspect of the American school curriculum, but typically it is a public relations-oriented forum for giving the school visibility in the community. Although some elementary schools have instrumental and vocal music programs, it is at the junior high school level that most schools initiate intensive music programs. At all levels of the American school system, the emphasis is placed on performances; Christmas and Easter holidays, graduations, and sporting events are celebrated by musical performances that usually are attended by the parents of the performers. Inevitably, there is considerable attention devoted to performing music that parents will enjoy rather than music that the students might choose or that the teachers feel can produce valid learning experiences.

Starting at the junior high school level, school band performances have dominated school music programs since the end of World War I.[1] In many communities, the school band is the recipient of much local pride and attention, and fund-raising events such as bake sales and raffles are used to earn the money to outfit the band in snappy uniforms, enter the band or chorus in local or regional contests competing against other school ensembles, or send the band to such media events as the Orange

or Rose bowls, with their national television coverage. On oc-
casion, high school ensembles compete in international contests
in Europe or South America. There are many similarities between
the music programs in the schools and the drills used in school
athletic programs.

Sports events and holiday celebrations constitute a vehicle for
mobilizing school spirit and increasing community support. There
is nothing intrinsically wrong in inculcating these value systems,
but they have little to do with music education or aesthetic experiences. The average school band musician, like the average
school athlete, ceases to play music after graduation.

Actually, there is a strong parallel to the athlete's experience.
The child who played football or basketball with joy and enthusiasm in elementary school and junior high finds in high school
or college that the average player has no place on the team. As
the competition gets stiffer, the ordinary junior or senior high
school singer or musician is eliminated from college ensembles.
These involuntarily retired athletes and musicians then become
spectators or consumers rather than producers of music. There
is little room in the school music program for enjoyment of music
for its own sake or as an activity designed to lead to personal
growth.

As a sometime guitar and banjo teacher, I have taught quite
a few former students who tooted their clarinets or flutes in the
school band. Many had not played music in twenty years. After
two or three beginning guitar lessions, they invariably came away
astounded that they could sing and play a simple accompaniment
to a song. The guitar and piano are polyphonic instruments,
capable of playing chords, and the average band musician has
never experienced playing a song without the band. All they did
in school was play an inner part to a football fight song, usually
doubled by a dozen other flute or clarinet players. Why should
an adult want to practice these parts once the marching band is
no longer part of his or her life?

Although average school band musicians may have achieved
a minimum of musical literacy in the school music program, they

have generally learned little or nothing about the process or the enjoyment of making music. School programs are generally not designed to deal with these issues. They are designed instead to handle large groups of people and to have them perform the rituals we associate with music, generally in connection with social events. The value of music making for its own sake is simply not part of the grand design.

School choral performances follow the same general outlines. They often include snappy choreography and performances of show tunes guaranteed to please the older generation. The costumes and choreography complete the parental illusion of seeing their children performing in a mini-Broadway show.

The musical performances I have been describing are more representative of the values of show business and the use of music as a commodity than of the purposes of music education. What the student learns in these performances is relevant to audience tastes, performance values, and the joys of travel, in short to everything but music. Often the same teachers who are in charge of these performances will discourage the students from playing rock or country music on the theory that these kinds of music are "simple" or "primitive." Throughout the high school and college music programs, a rather odd worship is afforded to large instrumental and vocal groups. Once again, the team element is a part of this validation process. We must also remember that instructing large groups of students with one teacher is a cost-effective measure that appeals to school administrators and governing bodies.

At present, there are two fundamental crisis areas that confront the music educator. First, there is the problem of declining population and decreasing school enrollment. As the school population diminishes and as the government becomes increasingly budget-minded, there are fewer teaching jobs available in school music programs. With the emphasis placed on justifying each nickel spent, the large number of students serviced by a single teacher makes the band and choral programs very attractive to administrators.

The other problem is the disparity between what is taught in school music programs and what the students are actually interested in learning and performing. Even when music educators try to meet these desires, they are often way off base. For example, in an effort to capitalize on the tremendous upsurge in the popularity of the guitar, many schools have introduced basic guitar classes. Many of the people teaching these programs are music specialists for whom the guitar is a third or fourth instrument, one that they have not studied formally. Such a teacher is often only a step ahead of the students. Also, although the students want to play current hit songs, they are usually taught to read the notes on each string of the guitar by playing such tunes as "Twinkle Twinkle Little Star." Student incentive and enthusiasm are thereby subverted into another "learn by the notes" musical experience. One way to stimulate school music programs can be to utilize musicians in the local community. However, because the requirements for teacher certification are strict, it is often impossible for the schools to use qualified people in the community to teach guitar programs unless they have achieved teacher certification status.

The unfortunate fact is that many high school and college music teachers are musical dilettantes who do not grasp the historical, aesthetic, or stylistic problems of music but simply try to mold their students to fulfill the band or choral-performance objectives that the community seems to value.[2] Student needs become secondary to the acquisition of virtuoso skills.

There is no evidence that this process is producing students who are more knowledgeable about music or have any grasp of the creative process itself.[3] Even the teaching of jazz in schools represents a technical process rather than a living and growing aesthetic based on Afro-American culture. Is there any point to teaching musical processes apart from teaching about the culture that forms the basis for the origin and development of these processes? The music teacher is often stronger on technique than on any understanding of the backgrounds of, say, jazz or the culture that created it. Music is thus reduced to a series of empty exercises rather than an expression of emotion that uses the development of technical skills as a tool to facilitate the emotional aspects of the performance. The development of technical skills is not synonymous with musicality or musical understanding, which is developed instead through a rich understanding of the roots of music and a comprehension of how these roots spread to other soil.

The use of American folk music and nonwestern music in the schools often fails on similar grounds. Folk music is presented as something quaint and primitive. The student is not led to an understanding of where the music came from, the streams that fed its development and growth, or the aesthetics that govern its performance. I have an unforgettable memory from the days when I was a student at the University of Colorado at Denver around 1975. I suggested to the head of the music department that a performance of a blues, in the style of a musician like Mississippi John Hurt, could be judged in a performance sense in the same way as a jazz solo or a piano performance of a Bach fugue. The teacher, who was far more open to a variety of musical styles than most college teachers, confessed that he personally did not possess a sufficient understanding of the aesthetics involved to be able to judge such a performance. How many colleges have ensembles that play rhythm and blues or country music? There are virtually none, yet every school has ensembles composed of such students who are working many nights of the week performing music. Most school music departments will not recognize these ensembles for credit hours for the simple reason that many of the musicians in these groups do not read music and often are not particularly interested in learning to do so.

As the pop song says, now we are down to the real nitty-gritty. If the Beatles could write all their songs without any formal knowledge of music, and if a music critic like Wilfred Mellers could do an extended analysis of their melodic invention and harmonic usage, how important are school music programs, and what is the relationship between musical talent and the way music is taught in the school system? The answers to these questions lead to the disclosure of the value systems of the teachers. For most music teachers, symphonic or jazz band music (depending on the teacher's background) is the acme of musical achievement, and popular music forms are simple and insignificant. The student inevitably feels that the teacher is saying, "Don't play your music, learn about ours." In fact, most school music teachers know very little about rock and roll, country, or folk music.

In the last thirty years or so, music education had gone through quite a few changes of thought and orientation, particularly in regard to the education of young children. The Orff and Kodaly systems were introduced from Europe, and from Japan came the Suzuki system of talent development. Suzuki takes children who are three or four years old and teaches them to play on miniature violins and cellos.[4] His system starts with simple exercises and ear training before progressing to music reading. Part of the Suzuki system aesthetic involves the use of parents as monitors at lessons and in practice sessions. Many of the parents have no previous musical skills or training, and so the lessons represent a learning experience for them as well.

Kodaly emphasized the teaching of technical skills to children in the primary schools through the study of Hungarian folk songs, starting with simple pentatonic (five-tone) melodies and progressing through a rigorous course of sight-singing and music reading. The Kodaly system has produced a marked increase in musical literacy in Hungary, and there is now a Kodaly Institute in Wellesley, Massachusetts.[5] Kodaly felt that all nations should emphasize the study of their own music in the teaching of children.

Carl Orff concentrated on involving children in rhythms and in building musical instruments that are easy for children to play. He also composed music for these instruments, and the sale of Orff instruments and music has become an industry in its own right. Quite a few music educators in the United States have combined aspects of the Orff and Kodaly systems in teaching music to young children.

Other systems that stress the use of movement and dance

alongside the development of musical skills have been in use in the United States for some time. The Dalcroze method includes a combination of music and dance called eurhythmics, and the Carabo Cone system stresses the development of motor coordination and physical skills in the learning of music. The Yamaha music schools offer group lessons for children in private studios. These lessons include movement, rhythm, and simple songwriting and improvisation.

The use of these methods has opened up a dialogue about the way people learn music that had been missing from the American educational scene. In the eighteenth and nineteenth centuries, music was regarded by educators as a sort of ethical and moral force connected to religious ideals. This gave way to the pragmatic marketing approach of performances by school music ensembles.[6] With the introduction of some of the techniques described in the paragraphs above, there is more of an emphasis in elementary school education on the way that children learn and on the idea that learning can be fun. There is less of the simple task orientation of learning to read music and follow a conductor.

With the introduction of the chorus and orchestra performance syndrome in junior high school, the benefits of a looser and more enlightened system of learning are dissipated. Let us consider how a junior or senior high school program can operate in such a way that it would relate to what the students want and at the same time create a stimulating learning environment leading to the development of musical skills. The first goal I envisage is to provide each student as broad a background in music as possible, given the neccessary limitations of the teachers' experiences and skill levels.

A remarkable book called *Pop Music in School*[7] describes the way popular music is integrated into the music program in a number of schools in England. The book is a collection of articles by several authors, most of whom seem to agree that the music teacher should begin with the apparent interests of the students. To a considerable extent, this means beginning with rock and roll, although in American schools the program might just as easily start with country music, blues, or folk music. An "open" music department makes use of student skills and the skills of teachers who are not necessarily in the music department. Other community resources include private music teachers, professional musicians, and amateur musicians with particular skills not found in the teaching staff.[8] The expertise of the students is used to help select a contemporary record library that represents the music that students are interested in learning. In many cases, the teachers are ignorant of the artists who perform on these records. The point is to get a representative sampling of the music that students like and find meaningful.

The open music program dictates that there must be quite a number of student ensembles of varying size playing different styles of music. The instrumentation begins with what the students are able to play. An extraordinary number of students at the high school or college level play the rhythm instruments found in rock and roll and country music, such as guitars, keyboard instruments, synethesizers, bass guitars, and drums. The open music program cannot have a formal syllabus because, of necessity, the program changes from day to day. Creativity and development are ongoing and continuous. This format does not include large orchestras or choral groups for students who want to participate in them. The point is to involve all students in the music program, whatever their musical preference.

Improvisation and composition are an intrinsic part of such a music program, and the teacher must be responsive to these processes. This involves many music teachers in a sort of massive self-education process, learning about popular music styles and trying to relate them to the formal teaching of music. The object is not to turn music teachers into authorities on popular music but to enable them to relate contemporary popular music to the formal styles in which they were trained. In an open musical environment, students will seek out more formal music training as an aid to their own work. For example, a student guitarist will hear a piano player using complicated chord patterns and will want to learn these chords. Another student may want a trumpet part on her song and may find that it is most efficient to write that part out for the player. This lesson may evolve when the singer allows the trumpet player to make up his own part, but when that part is not satisfactory for her tastes she may be inspired to write the part herself.

On the other hand, many formally trained musicians can learn interesting lessons about rhythm, timbre, musical energy, and improvisation from popular music.[9] In much contemporary popular music, the harmonic structure is secondary to considerations of timbre, tone color, volume, and texture. The question of what constitutes a "good" sound on the guitar has a different answer for rock, jazz, and classical guitarists. The sheer volume and energy of certain rock forms can produce interesting musical results once the teacher gets over the initial discomfort of the volume level.

From 1978 to 1981, I worked as a teacher in suburban Denver high schools in a project called Popular Music as a Creative Process. This project was designed to teach high school students to write songs, arrange them for recording, and operate the recording equipment. The project culminated in a twelve-inch LP record during the first year of the project and some additional recordings in the following two years. There were three music teachers involved in the project including myself, none of whom were certified to teach in Colorado. We worked separately and together on lyric writing, melody writing, record production, and performance. In the first year we worked at the Mountain Open Living High School in Evergreen, Colorado, a school with no formal music program. One of the teachers employed by the school was an excellent flute player who had studied quite a bit of music, and some other teachers at the school enrolled in the program as students just to see what would happen.

The program was quite successful. In a period of four months, the students wrote, arranged, and recorded a dozen songs, and one student even supervised the writing of a song on a school trip that did not involve any of the three teachers. Many of the students who vowed that they had no musical or writing talents ended up writing lyrics, playing musical instruments, singing, and participating in decisions as to which performances were best. Other students operated the recording equipment, a portable four-track tape recorder with inexpensive microphones and speakers.

Very few of the students had any previous musical training. One student was a classically trained violinist who had never dared to improvise. We were able to provide her with a context in which she could afford to take chances and learn from listening to her own recorded performances. I particularly remember one student who sang, wrote lyrics and melodies, and seemed able to pick up any musical instrument that was lying around and play at least a musical phrase or two on it. He played trumpet, mandolin, guitar, bass, and percussion in the course of making the record. Watching this student try his musical wings made me think about the nature of creativity and musical training. How could someone continually pick up musical instruments and play them when he had no clear idea of what he was doing? It began to occur to me that no one had ever told Jerrold that he could not play these instruments and that consequently, he approached them with the assumption that he could.

Imagine the possibilities if we approached music education this way. Rather than telling prospective students about all the tasks they were going to have to fulfill—reading music, sight-singing, learning harmony and theory, and the like—suppose we approached each musical instrument or task as a challenge that we expected students to meet and enjoy. It is probably this lack of confidence in the student population that is such an inhibiting factor in music classes, lessons, and even parental attitudes toward the study and mastery of music.

Evergreen, Colorado, is a fairly prosperous and middle-class town with a predominantly white population. In other musical environments, we need to utilize the musical skills and interests of the student population. I have a friend named Jack La Fort who teaches music in a Chicano section of Denver. He tells me that when his band plays anything, the percussion section adds some amazing Latin rhythms, picking up the spirit of the band. Another teacher would very likely try to force these percussionists into a more formal mold, but Jack gets a kick out of their rhythmic improvisations. He is an excellent jazz saxophone player, but he admits that he would never have come up with these rhythms on his own. When students learn about jazz in a high school or college classroom, they need to learn about the blues and gospel roots of the music and the sufferings and difficulties that jazz musicians encounter. To teach students to play arrangements bought from a New York music publisher with no understanding of where the music comes from is senseless and cheats the students of an education.

The roots of rock and roll include such diverse musical and cultural elements as country music, folk music, soul music, West Indian, folk, and gospel music. Each of these styles provides chances to teach about fascinating aspects of American culture and even the cultures of Africa and India. When I was asked to teach a college course called "Music Cultures of the World," I found that most of my students were appallingly ignorant of Afro-American history and culture. I in turn needed to study the history, politics, and culture of African and Asian societies so that I could understand the music that came out of those societies.

In every school environment there is some minority group or some musical style that could capture the interest of the students, provided that the teacher does not insist upon subordinating this music to some preconceived notion of the way a band should perform. Classical music has its varied environments as well, and the study of court musicians, electronic music, or atonality can provide students with a great deal of insight into historical and cultural processes.

If this kind of stimulation is not available in the student population, it may be present in the community itself. Parents, church groups, and professional musicians who do not work in the school, along with records and videotapes, can provide further musical influences for the students. This music should be integrated into units on social science, history, and geography through team teaching. This should stimulate a creative interchange of ideas about music and other subject-centered areas.

The college music program presents its own set of difficulties. Three basic music programs are available in colleges and music conservatories. There is a B.A. in music, which is general humanities-based education with some forty to fifty hours of music study. The B.M. degree offered by many universities requires sixty to seventy hours of music study, and there are degree programs offered by music schools like the Juilliard School or the Curtis Institute. These latter programs include only about fifteen to twenty hours of study outside music. All of these figures are part of a total program that includes from one hundred twenty to one hundred twenty-five hours of college credit. The standard B.A. program includes two years of music theory and harmony, counterpoint, individual lessons in one instrument, ensemble playing and singing, and often a keyboard proficiency exam. The B.M. degree adds more hours in the student's major instrument and in music history and has much stiffer ensemble requirements than the B.A. generally does. The third music degree that is available in many college music programs is a degree in music education. To acquire this degree, the student must take twenty additional hours in education in addition to the required hours in music. Degrees in music therapy or the music industry operate on the same principle, adding psychology and business hours, respectively, in addition to the basic music hours.

The assumption governing all the college programs is that the two-year theory, history, sight-singing, and the lessons program forms the basic materials of a music education, and additional requirements are added according to the student's area of concentration. Stage bands that perform jazz or rock-jazz fusion music are popular in many colleges. Once again, the focus is on performance and on exposure for the college's music program. The atmosphere of the college music department does not encourage the exploration of new musical territory or acknowledge the vitality of popular music. True improvisation is probably too close to musical anarchism and too removed from formal, codified training for a college music program to accept it.[10] It is much safer to practice technique and to do formal analyses of classical music or jazz than to actually explore the music itself.

When I was a music student at the University of Colorado at Denver in 1972–75, I started to write musical arrangements for the college stage band. I wrote a fifteen-piece arrangement loosely based on the old square dance tune "Cripple Creek" that included two banjo parts. I asked the teacher who conducted the band if he would conduct the piece, since I was playing one of the banjo parts. He was quite busy sorting parts from a Buddy Rich big band arrangement from *West Side Story*, and he demurred, suggesting that I conduct it myself. I had some difficulty conducting the piece while playing, but I gave it a try. In the middle of the arrangement, there was a trumpet improvisation, which I assigned to the trumpet player who I felt was the most flexible musician in the band. To my horror, out came a 1950 bebop solo. I suddenly realized that to many musicians, improvisation is a synonym for a particular style of jazz rather than an approach to music that is dictated by the stylistic demands of the particular idiom in which the piece is written.

It was startling to comprehend that although my piece did not represent any remarkable musical innovations, hardly anyone in the band seemed to have a basic understanding of what I was attempting. The teacher fulfilled the role of what I would call noneducation; he ignored something that he failed to understand, instead of offering support or criticism.

The UCLA music department has a number of ensembles that play nonwestern music. Some of the players come from the music department, and quite a few are students at UCLA who are interested in various musical styles. In my opinion, this is the way a college music department should be run—encouraging participation from all interested students, not just music majors. Unfortunately, in most college programs there may be separate jazz, classical, folklore, and ethnomusicology programs, with little cross-fertilization between them. Each one has its own jealously guarded territory.

A music program at a college should take students through every style of music imaginable, with some attempt to play music, discuss performance criteria, and even write music in those styles. At every college there are students who never step inside the music department who may well be the most talented musicians in the school from the standpoint of experimentation, open-mindedness, and the willingness to take compositional and performance risks. These are values that few college music programs communicate to the students. There should be more programs designed around individual needs and talents rather than the same drab standardized requirements.

More colleges should offer courses on the history and development of popular music alongside the obligatory jazz survey course that represents the only tribute that most music departments are willing to pay to contemporary popular music. Songwriting should be offered to students, possibly team-taught by a music professor and a member of the journalism or literature departments. A music education degree should include courses in songwriting, improvisation, and the history of American folk music.

We live in an era in which the music of the entire world is available to us on records and live in many cities through the performances of resident ethnic groups. It should be the function of the music curriculum to utilize the music of this kaleidoscope of world culture to stimulate the students. Through the Orff and Kodaly methods, there is probably more of this process going on in the lower grades of the American school system than in the higher educational ranks, which still focus on performing ensembles that will bring publicity to the school. We need to be more concerned about the needs and interests of the students and less about the traditional desires of parents and teachers. By including popular music in junior and senior high school programs, we can involve more students in music programs and stimulate an interchange of ideas between students and teachers. The teacher's role should be to find out what interests the student and to show the student how this interest can relate to formal music in terms of composition, arrangement, or musical invention. The students' ethnic heritage and musical experiences should be the cornerstone of the school music program rather than an afterthought thrown in to appease the students. Through shared musical experiences, attempted improvisations, and compositions, the music program can come to life and present an infinite number of challenges for students and teachers. This will avoid the calculated duplication of annual Christmas programs and football game serenades, although it will not necessarily eliminate them.

Televised music instruction and videotaped lessons and performances can provide an exciting ingredient for the enrichment of school programs. Some states, such as Georgia, already have instituted broad-based television shows to expose students to various forms of music.[10] We can easily imagine a time when student ensembles will be able to make records and videotapes and when these products will be circulated through community-access cable television or educational television. It should be understood that the members of an ensemble do not necessarily have to read music to play well. Notation is a tool for facilitating musical communication, not a synonym for music.

The average child should be encouraged to make music whether or not he or she fits into the school orchestra or chorus. Popular music is a perfect place to mobilize the musical creativity of such students. They should be encouraged in the exploration of their musical skills rather than condescended to, as so many music programs seem to feel is necessary. Songwriting, improvisation, and the history and aesthetics of popular music should all be part of the school music program, and they should be treated as seriously as any other musical areas.

If we use the technology available to us, the school music program can be made exciting, fulfilling, and experimental. There is room for every kind of music and for the development of skills within each style. All we need to do is educate the teachers.

OPENING ACTS:
The Infantry of Rock and Roll*

by Artie Traum

Artie Traum is a singer, guitarist, songwriter, and record producer. He has recorded and toured widely, and in this article, re-printed from The Oak Report, he discusses his career as an "opening act," for some of the top pop and rock music performers.

I've just come home from another tour, having driven 2,168 miles in ten days, to "open" concerts for Pure Prairie League, Livingston Taylor and the Dirt Band. My partner and I spent sixty-five hours in the car, and a meager six hours on stage. This absurd ratio makes us feel more like truck drivers than musicians, with a "forty-five minute set" the product we deliver. Most of the concerts were held in huge gymnasiums in colleges tucked away in the rolling hills of Pennsylvania, Ohio and New York. They all harbored similar charms designed to deflate the most resilient artistic ego: smelly locker rooms to practice in, watery lasagna for dinner and a host of freshman clones who always manage to bungle the easiest tasks. College tours seem to take the "show" our of show business, and, when you are an opening act, business is never booming either.

Opening acts, (aka warm-up bands) are the infantry of the pop music world. The job calls for true military strategy: take the stage, dig in and hold it for forty-five minutes. If you can subdue the audience for that long, you get a check; if you retreat from a barrage of boos and catcalls, you also get a check. Soldiers get paid, win or lose.

I've been an opening act for over fifteen years. Sometimes I think I must be crazy to practice my art in situations that conjure up military metaphors. If that sentiment seems extreme, consider this: a steamy July evening in New York's Central Park several years ago. My brother, Happy, and I are waiting backstage to open a show for The Band. The arena is sold out. Several thousand fans can't get in and they are pushing at the gates. Security is worried. Bottles are being tossed. One shatters in the backstage area. A security guard positions himself on top of the crowded backstage trailer and shouts "Incoming!" as we duck for cover. Ron Delsner, the promoter, begs us to play. We rush the stage, plug in our instruments and begin our set without a chance to tune up.

Luckily, New York was our home town, and we had our own fans dotting the audience. They knew that we were the sacrificial lambs, but they weren't about to let the crowd shed one drop of our musical blood. To top off the show, Levon Helm and Rick Danko came out to sing harmony with us, and the crowd went wild. Nothing like having a star join you to make you a credible performer. Audiences love credentials; you are a nothing, a nobody, until you can prove otherwise.

A few weeks later we weren't so lucky. Capitol Records, trying to get us massive exposure in Philadelphia, squeezed us in on a Led Zepplin, Grand Funk Railroad heavy metal concert in an outdoor city park. We arrived early, parked our rented car at the edge of the crowd (about 10,000 fans, and not our fans) and walked to the stage. We felt very jittery about opening a rave-up rock show with an acoustic band, and watching the headliners arrive by helicopter was no consolation. Our first song met with scattered applause, the second drew less, and after the third song there was no response. We weren't heckled. We weren't booed. Just a sea of faces peering at us as though we'd arrived from Pluto. There is nothing worse than audience indifference. It leaves you hanging, wondering what you did wrong or how you can change the set to get through. I'd much rather incite hostility since that's an energy you can *feel*, and even work with. I decided to try an idea that was at best a long shot. I borrowed a guitar from one of the bands, turned the volume to deafening, and played every heavy metal lick I knew, tossing in quotes from Hendrix, Clapton, Beck, Harrison and Page. I strutted across the stage, dropped down to my knees and bent strings until my fingers burned. Then, before the audience could figure out what was going on, we left the stage. The crowd (which had grown to over 100,000) was shouting for more as we made our way to the car. The car had been crushed to scrap metal by fans who claimed they were "liberating" it. It didn't seem like D-Day to us, so we reclaimed it and shuttled it back to the folks at Avis. They never understood.

Opening concerts is almost always a thankless task, but it rarely gets boring. The best part of all is meeting and hanging out with some of the best musicians in the world. The worst part is losing an audience when one's fellow musicians are watching in the wings. They can always console you, however, with some story about *their* experiences as an opening act. Everyone is an opening act at some time. My current partner, Pat Alger, and I have opened shows for the popular rock band Orleans. We never seem to reach their crowd, but lead singer Larry Hoppen always tells me the story of their Allman Brothers concert.

Orleans, riding the crest of their hit single "Love Takes Time," opened for the Allmans at a huge arena in Rochester, New York. If Orleans is popular, the Allmans are legendary. Opening their high energy set, Larry was shocked by the response: "The first few rows were yelling at us and making obscene gestures, and waves of booing came from the rest of the crowd. I mean, how can you do a show with that going on?"

John Sebastian, former leader of the Lovin' Spoonful, was touring to promote his monstrously successful hit "Welcome Back" when he got an opening slot with comedian Steve Martin. Before the first show, he stole a peek at the audience. "Do you know what it's like," he asked me recently, "to see five thousand people with toy arrows through their heads?" John is an experienced, veteran (another military reference) peformer, and he went out to meet this audience. He won their adulation almost every night, but he always knew it was touch and go.

When you see a star like Steve Martin in the spotlight, it's hard to believe that he was an opening act himself for a long time. A few years ago I traveled as an opening act for Martin, who opened for Linda Ronstadt, who opened for the Nitty Gritty Dirt Band. Our first show was in a lovely outdoor theater in Sante Fe. I did a very short, energetic set. Steve Martin was as crazy as I've ever seen him, climbing to the roof of the stage, appearing in the audience and generally creating an atmosphere of irresistible madness. Linda, not yet a superstar, paced nervously backstage, wedged between Steve and the Dirt Band. What a performance she gave! Those of us who felt chills when she sang "Heart Like a Wheel" had no idea of the insecurity that plagued her before she went on stage.

Pop music is a shifting hierarchy, with superstars finding themselves quite expendable in the kingdom. It may be the only profession besides sports in which tenure decreases with age; in which middle age is feared and dreaded because it turns today's hero into a has-been. From an opening act's point of view it's better to be a has-been than, in the words of songwriter George Gerdes, a "never-was." A former star with a decent accountant can parlay a past success into a thriving publishing or production business. But if he's blown his money on booze, drugs or credit-card dinners, he might find himself touring before distracted audiences half his age, just to meet the rent. There are more than a few of these performers around, drinking cheap wine after years of *eau de vie.*

All performers want, more than anything, the respect of their peers, and success or failure with an audience is magnified if a fellow musician is watching. An opening act experiences great frustration making the compromises needed to reach an audience. I find I have to throw in snappy one-liners, crowd pleasers and jokes just to keep an audience's attention. I don't have a backlog of hit records that are applauded after the first measure. It's a disappointing task to know you can tap only a small part of your talent, since so much energy is just going into surviving the set. Invariably, I feel I have to apologize to the headliner about the quality of the music, and have the haunting feeling that the depth of my abilities is lost in the shuffle.

If it's so bad out there, why do performers open shows? Two reasons: money and exposure. Money is usually minimal and exposure is questionable, since introductions to the crowd are often forgotten or simply wrong. Think of how it feels to watch the president of student activities announce you so poorly that you don't even know he's just introduced you! Still, competition for opening spots has the fierceness of sharks in a feeding frenzy. In fact, many top showcase clubs in major cities charge acts to use their stage. This charge is usually paid for by record companies, which buy radio and print ads, guarantee ticket sales and wine and dine scores of people at the club's bar. The band is also supported by the record company in the form of "tour support"—money advanced against future royalties to cover expenses on the road. A five-piece band, carrying a four-man crew, can easily cost upwards of one thousand dollars a day. With the inflationary economy of the last few years, many successful bands have stopped touring, and tour support to opening acts is being cut off. Recording companies are reluctant to underwrite a tour that may add $50,000 to a recording budget that could easily have cost three times that. A band, or artist, with tour support has the moral support of the crew, manager and big corporation behind him. Without it, many performers crumble fast.

As dismal as they may seem, college concerts are the *crème de la crème* for opening acts. Student activity fees can occasionally cough up as much as $2,500 for an opening act with a name, such as Liv Taylor or Loudon Wainwright. Generally, concert committees will reserve only $250 to $500 for that slot. Often, a local band will open the show, but more often a major agency will "force" an act on, saying, "If you want Band A to headline, you'll have to take Band B." This is called "clout" in the music business, and without it an artist's chances of working steadily are very slim. I've been bumped off concert tours by major agencies even after contracts have been signed—that's how powerful they can be.

Assuming you are lucky enough to get on the concert, you are likely to endure disrespect from that point on. More often than I care to remember, our names were left off the posters, or misspelled, or we simply were called "Special Guest." This gives me a feeling of being invisible, especially compared to the outrageously deferential treatment reserved for the headliner. While gofers are running to fetch ice or mustard or towels for the stars, it's all I can do to get a glass of water after the set. I've come to demand respect, I admit, with somewhat of a chip on my shoulder. I've been misused and abused too many times to take it lightly any longer.

Even under the best of circumstances, an opening act is under intense pressure. John McEwen, a show-stopping virtuoso with the Dirt Band, often opens for his own band. Audiences that force him from the stage are shocked to see that he is one of the players they'd come to see. If you survive an audience, you still have to survive the headliner. In a world of ever-vigilant egos, stars often feel threatened by an up-and-coming performer. I never knew the reason, but I once saw an irate headliner close the curtain again and again on a jazz-pop singer named Michael Franks. More often, a headliner will try to ease things for an opening act, by doing the introductions himself or interceding with a hostile audience in the middle of a set.

What happens when an opening act wipes the headliner off the stage? When Blood, Sweat and Tears first got started as a band, no one could follow them. Their horn arrangements, powerful rhythm section and haunting tunes left their audience spellbound, even before they cut their first album. I also once saw a shy, humble Kris Kristoffersen do the same thing many years ago at the Newport Folk Festival. Up against such luminaries as Joni Mitchell, Richie Havens and Taj Mahal, Kris ambled out onto the stage, strummed his guitar and knocked everybody out with the first performance of "Me and Bobby McGee." There was no glitter, no showmanship, no fancy singing or picking, but somehow Kris touched our hearts.

Kris's triumph at Newport holds a clue to why we continue performing. Although the industry dangles a golden carrot before our eyes (platinum records, worldwide acclaim), we know we are not likely to ever reach it. It's the small triumphs, the good nights, the occasional fan or admirer that keeps us going, and keeps us willing to forgive the thankless tasks.

With promoters suddenly disappearing into the crowd, the hunt for the check can be the last straw in a long day. They never seem to offer the money—they love to make you ask. How many times have I craved a nice seven-foot "roadie," someone to make me feel worthwhile and bring the little comforts that mean so much, like collecting the money at the end of the evening. Once the check is firmly secured in your wallet, you can look forward to an evening's peace at the nearest Holiday Inn, where you reflect on whether it's all been worth it.

Artie Traum's article raises a number of issues of vital importance to performing musicians and observers of American popular music. If anything, he underestimates the contrast between the success of top rock and roll performers and the day-to-day struggle of undiscovered musicians. In October 1981, the Rolling Stones played two afternoons in Boulder, Colorado. They left town with approximately $1 million, which represented the bulk of the money that was paid by almost 120,000 spectators. When an act is as famous as the Stones, the warm-up groups are performers who would be headliners in a smaller auditorium. The opening acts for the Stones' two shows were Heart and George Thorogood and the Destroyers. Each of these groups has been successful enough to have recorded hit singles or albums, but in this context they were opening acts. To Artie's description of the endless miles of driving I would like to add that even medium-priced acts like Livingston Taylor invariably fly from one job to the next, leaving their extensive road crews to transport speakers, lights, amplifiers, and other accessories from one city to the next by truck.

The analogy to military campaigns can be enlarged upon if we consider the use of security forces and doctors at large rock concerts. At a stadium rock concert, it is assumed that there will be arrests for the sale or use of drugs, overindulgence in alcohol, or the occasional act of violence. Rock promoters often provide their own security forces and beef them up with city policemen. An unruly concert may produce far worse results if, for example, the audience tries to storm the stage area. Security forces also eliminate gate crashing. Doctors or medical teams are often hired to treat such ailments as drug overdoses, alcohol abuse, or injuries. The use of extensive security forces or medical teams is not necessary at a typical college concert but is common practice at concerts in large stadiums or giant municipal auditoriums.

The most serious problem faced by the opening act is to keep a balance between what the audience may want to hear and what the performers want to present. This may be impossible, because the fans want to see the headline act. If the performer panders to the tastes of the audience with warmed-over hot guitar licks or tricky choreography, he or she may end up with a feeling of utter cynicism towards the music and the audience as well. I once read an interview with Neil Young in which he described performing as a process in which the audience spent the first ten minutes deciding whether it liked the performer. During that ten-minute period, Neil felt that the audience had stopped listening to the music and was simply reacting to the personality of the performer. For someone who devotes a great deal of time and energy to playing music, such as attitude is truly appalling.

Artie answers the question of why a performer continues to play music in the face of such disinterest by describing a few magic moments in which an audience discovered a new performer. My feeling is that most performers retain some sort of fantasy of future success. They continue to hope for, or expect, discovery by an audience or an important impresario in the midst of a college concert in Ogalalla, Nebraska, or some equally obscure place. From there the dream road becomes clear and includes hit records, sellout performances, lots of money, and artistic fulfillment. These dreams are almost always unrealistic, but they provide reinforcement for the elaborate mechanisms of the American popular music industry, which Joni Mitchell has called "the starmaker machinery behind the popular song."

MUZAK AND THE LISTENER

Imagine a world without the sounds of machinery: no refrigerators humming through the night, no alarm clocks buzzing, no whir of air-conditioners or telephones ringing or fluorescent lights droning—only the noises of wind and rain or people speaking to one another. This would constitute an unreal soundscape by the standards of the modern era.

Some of the feeling of ownership of sound, of hearing sounds that are intentional rather than packaged, can be created by paying attention to what sound is and what it does. In other words, voluntary listening is quite different from the experience of having sound inflicted upon you. I have known several families that always keep the television set on in their houses regardless of whether anyone is watching. It becomes an electronic massage, a reliable baby-sitter that never complains, and a companion for anyone in the family who is lonely.

My guess is that with the television off, all these people would feel better when they are awake, sleep better at night, and have more energy. I have walked into too many houses that play brainless background music as an accompaniment to everything—music that is not quite identifiable, sounds that are familiar but not quite experienced or cared about. Children do homework while listening to the radio or watching television, and dentists drill teeth while dulcet strings are playing "Tenderly." As the airplane is about to take off, in the background "soothing" music is jangling our nerves: a little message from the airlines to tell us that the airplane won't crash. Bus lines and many businesses put us on hold as background music plays dully and incessantly, interrupted only by a taped voice that periodically informs us that we shouldn't hang up and call again or we will lose our place in the rotation. I recall music at a motel swimming pool in El Paso droning on all night, softly and mindlessly. No one was at the pool late at night, but the bizarre orchestra continued its flaccid serenade. Muzak is in the supermarket as we shop, in some department stores, in restaurants, hotels and elevators, and at work.

Airlines, railroads, and city transportation systems all use Muzak when they place the caller on hold for minutes at a time. There is something particularly irritating about being captive to another's musical tastes that exceeds the annoyance of waiting for the ticket agent to come on the line.*

Let us not forget industry. Do you want your workers to be more productive? Play Muzak during the hours when we know workers tend to get drowsy. We can program the tunes in order of ascending stimulus value.[1] Translated into English, this means that as the workers get mentally or physically tired, we give them a shot of musical amphetamine, toe-tapping music to help them make it through the day. Keep the workers cheerful, and keep those widgets flowing on the assembly line. The computer programs a sprinkling of tunes that the worker recognizes: "Yesterday," "April in Paris," "Moonlight in Vermont." The tunes are not repeated too often, and once in a while they throw in a Muzak original, a tune written in the style of some old favorite but with a melodic turn or two that's just a trifle different.

Studies show that Muzak can speed up breathing, typing, and buying, delay fatigue, and improve attention and production. Other uses of Muzak are intended to promote relaxation and

* Thanks to Edith Friedlander for suggesting this line of thought.

induce a feeling of security. This sort of programming can be heard before an airplane takes off or at the doctor's office. There are thirty thousand tunes in the Muzak computer, and three hundred are added every year.[2] There is no hard rock, no funk, no hard-core anything. Usually there are no vocal solos, only instrumental music with some occasional vocal backgrounds. In Nova Scotia, schools have even used background music in the classroom.[3] Murray Schafer, in his book *The Tuning of the World*, says that "Moozak* is music that is not to be listened to."[4]

Muzak is a way of disguising the conditions of life in order to make the unacceptable acceptable. No one wants to be sitting in a dentist's chair; Muzak sends out the news that everything is okay. The airlines do not want us to be thinking about the remote, though real, possibility that our plane may crash. Apparently, the rationale is that if we are anaesthesized with music, we will not worry so much about what is happening to us. In restaurants and hotels, background music is supposed to create some sort of suave ambience that is associated with "class." Industrial Muzak or grocery Muzak makes us work harder or shop faster.

Muzak is a trade name for a particular corporation, although there are other services offering background music. The Muzak Corporation offers brochures that indicate rises in the productivity rate of workers in rooms where Muzak is played. A brochure entitled "Muzak Improves Productivity," asserts that tests at the Black and Decker plant in Hampstead, Maryland, show an increase in worker productivity of 2.80 percent when Muzak was installed. Muzak is the only background music service that records its own music, music that is not available on records or on the radio. The actual audio equipment may be bought or leased from Muzak, and the programming must be leased from the company. At the flip of a dial, the background music is immediately available.

When I was a traveling musician working with a pop-folk group called the Journeymen, John Phillips, the leader of the group,

---

* "Moozak" is Schaefer's own term.

and his girl friend, Michelle Gilliam, decided to get married. We were working in a club in Washington, D.C., and they found a justice of the peace in nearby Maryland. Scott Mackenzie and I, the other members of the group, were the only guests at the wedding. As the justice of the peace was reading the ceremony, Scott and I looked at each other. We knew that something was strange, but we couldn't identify it. Suddenly we both grinned. We realized simultaneously that the justice of the peace had not turned off his FM radio, which was playing the FM equivalent of Muzak—background music featuring a large string orchestra. John got married to the strains of Mantovani playing in the background, while Scott and I tried valiantly not to collapse with laughter.

Perhaps the ultimate tribute to the success of Muzak is that some radio stations have actually adopted its format in their programming. These stations play music that is quite similar to what is heard in Muzak, and the announcers and commercials are also generally low-key. There are differing MOR, or "middle of the road," radio formats. Some play relatively soft music by such artists as Frank Sinatra, Peggy Lee, and Tony Bennett, together with the softer contemporary rock sounds. At these stations, disc jockeys are at least allowed to have individual personalities. The oddest MOR station I ever heard was KABL, broadcasting in the San Francisco area in the mid-1960s. The announcers all spoke in muffled voices that the station manager must have thought were sensual, and they talked incessantly about the fog rolling in across San Francisco Bay. Other MOR stations, usually FM stations, imitate the Muzak format. Some of these stations are automated. The station purchases tapes from a radio production company, such as TM Productions in Dallas, and runs the tapes twenty-four hours a day. Some stations hire one or two local announcers who break in with the news and weather every hour, while others are entirely automated.

My favorite automated format was an FM station in Denver that asked for listener requests. Once in a while the caller asked for a tune that was coming up on the tape anyway; usually the poor receptionist had to pretend that the station didn't have the record or couldn't find it. The automated background music station represents the ultimate triumph of Muzak over disc jockeys, with their personalized raps, silly jokes, and local references. Radio can function in the same way as background music: soothing listeners, increasing their energy level, and not making any demands on their attention span or intelligence. Why bother with real people at a radio station? Tape is cheaper.

Given the complex and contradictory nature of our society, it was almost inevitable that some sort of musical device would come into being that represented values that are directly opposite to the values of background music. The most obvious example is the rectangular portable FM-AM radio cassette player, or "black box." These toys have appeared all over the streets of New York and in many other cities. Most of these cassette-radios are quite large and can be played at high volume levels. They are often used in situations in which there are crowds of people who do not know one another, and they are almost invariably owned by teenagers.

These black boxes create some fascinating social interactions. Start with the assumption that most adults do not like loud music, specifically loud rock and roll or disco music. Often the owners of the black boxes are black or Chicano teenagers who are listening to their favorite music while middle-aged, middle-class white adults are cringing in the foreground or background. It is as though the kids were saying: "I know you don't like me, and you don't like my music, but now you are not going to be able to ignore my tastes, because I am going to impose them on you." There is also an inplied dare that the teenager is making to the adult: "Hey, man, just try and ask me to turn the volume down. Just try it." The implication is that such a move will lead to violence or an argument, both very embarrassing if not threatening to the typical adult in a group situation with a crowd of people who do not know one another and have no particular reason to offer support. It is a rare individual who will accept this challenge.

Let us take this process a step further. If Muzak is intended to be unobtrusive, to escape one's notice but produce a carefully calculated result such as better production in the office, then the actions of the teenager are intended to achieve a direct and quick reaction of anger, hostility, argument, and an acknowledgment of the teenager's existence on the part of the adult. Instead of the soundscape being controlled by the corporate smoothie, it is being taken over by the hostile teenager. What the teenager wants is to be noticed, perhaps to be disliked, to dignify his or her place in the world. For some years, all record producers of teenage music have been pursuing a similar course: Make the music as loud as possible so that kids can get off on their parents hating the music. The same ethic relates to hair styles, bizarre clothing, or drugs—anything, in short, that parents will dislike. However, this is not a family situation but a potentially explosive incident, because the people do not know one another. The hostility is not a familial game but represents a cultural conflict based upon differences in values and the question of what is socially acceptable, what is forbidden, and what is best ignored. My friend Larry Sandberg makes the interesting point that the black boxes define the turf of the owner in a sort of classic teenage gangland style. The black boxes, by the way, don't come cheap. They are priced in the $200 to $500 range, and they have loud-speakers that are not easily ignored. A business must pay to lease Muzak, but it is free to the consumer of the music. The teenager has literally paid a heavy price to assert individual musical and personal values.

A more recent development are the personal portable FM radio-cassette players such as the Sony Walkman. These machines are designed so that the owner walks around with headphones, hearing the rough equivalent of what one can hear at home on a stereo set. The differences between the personal portable and the black box are interesting. The black box compels everyone within earshot to hear the same sounds that the owner is hearing. The personal portable deliberately excludes anyone but the owner from listening, because there is only one input for the headphones. Instead of the macho-aggressive aspects that define the use of the black box, we have a thoroughly respectable passive hostility here. We get the impression that Walkman owners don't want to share the soundscape with the rest of us. They appear almost smug, lost in their own world of music or fantasy.

There is a social statement here, too, of course, albeit one that is easier for the spectator to accept. Sometimes this statement is accentuated by other solipsistic habits of some of the personal portable people. There are the gaudily dressed skaters, headphones pressed to their ears while roller skating in full regalia, and there are the bicyclists and automotive headphone freaks who seem dangerously oblivious to any sound outside their earplugs.

Stores, restaurants, and clubs that deal with teenagers and young adults use a modification of the black box method. In rock-oriented record stores, loud music comes out of giant speakers at all times. The clerks groove appropriately to the music with their body language, wearing appropriate T-shirts that celebrate rock groups. Similarly, clothing stores that cater to the young play loud music from FM rock stations. The consumer gets the message: Older folks go home; welcome young set. I have watched middle-aged adults in these "hip" record stores, looking furtively around them, holding their ears and trying to get the attention of the cool clerks. An older person is thoroughly uncomfortable in this teenage environment that has been carefully packaged by the corporate mind to maximize record sales with the young set. It always seems to be the corporation, aided by market researchers and media experts, that sets the rules of the game. In some business situations, refined background music and soft lights set the tone. If more dollars can be made with blaring rock and light shows, a record store will go with that approach.

Looking at these musical and social modes tells us a great deal about the musical tastes and social tensions that exist in contemporary society. Muzak is music for people who don't have much personal feeling for music. The listener wants only to hear something that is familiar, "pretty," soothing, and unthreatening. The melody of any tune played on Muzak is always clearly defined. There is seldom anything complex in the musical arrangements, and the rhythmic patterns are simple. Muzak rock sounds more like Eddie Fisher than Fleetwood Mac. No fuzz-tone guitars, no buzzing synthesizers, and no pounding drums are allowed. Muzak is lyrical in a thoroughly simplistic way, like a Keane painting or a Rod McKuen poem. No one will have trouble understanding this kind of music. Whatever the client wants—to make the assembly line move faster or to take the patient's mind off his or her pain—is the goal of background music. What the listener may prefer to hear is irrelevant.

The experience of living in the real world is not always pleasant. Birth, growing up, sickness, work, dying—all these experiences cannot always be pleasant and innocuous. What are we being protected against? Feeling anything? Perhaps the role of background music is to protect us against listening to anything or anyone. If we listen to music or to what people say, we may become happy, sad, overwhelmed, or moved to tears. Any of a thousand other personal emotional feelings may surface, some of them intangible and perhaps even inexplicable. Playing music that does not require us to listen constitutes a major inroad on our ability to be human, to live and think and feel. How can we experience pleasure if we are unable to experience pain? On the physical or psychological level, we have doctors who are always ready to provide us with a drug-induced calm, whether the experience to be overcome is childbirth, terminal cancer, or the common cold. Muzak is drug-like music, a pill to induce productivity, dull pain, and reduce perception.

As obnoxious as the black boxes are or can be they represent an assertion of life in contrast to the fundamental nothingness of Muzak. The black box announces: "I care about my music, and I am going to make you care about me. Even if this means you are going to hate me." So long live the black box, and long live rock and roll and disco or country music if the listener cares about them. Has anyone ever cared about Muzak? Do people go into the local record store and buy a record just like the Muzak they have heard at the local factory or restaurant? As for the personal portables, why not? I am not sure that shutting oneself into an individual soundscape that exists outside any external reality is healthy, but at least it represents an assertion of personal choice. Ultimately, background music represents aspects of intellectual fascism, for it is music chosen for us by someone else that we are compelled to listen to, whatever our preferences.

I have chosen not to discuss the question of what it means for people to have to listen to music at very high levels of volume. Clearly, it is becoming difficult to hear anything in our urban environment. Listening loud is certainly not to be interpreted as listening better, closer, or more acutely. But it does constitute an active position, as opposed to the passive role of the victim of canned music.

If everyone who read this article decided not to put up with Muzak, there wouldn't be any background music. Next time you are in the doctor's office, tell the doctor that the background music is disturbing you. When you get on an airplane, ask the cabin attendant to turn the background music down or off. Try to persuade your children to study without background music. If you are not watching television or listening to the radio, don't keep them on. Listeners of the world, revolt; you have nothing to lose but your background music.

THE MUSICIANS' UNION IN
THE 1980s

The American Federation of Musicians (AFM) is the largest talent union in North America. It represents people who play musical instruments, whereas other talent unions represent singers, actors, comedians, or jugglers. AGMA, the American Guild of Musical Artists, shares jurisdiction of concert artists with the AFM. The AFM has six hundred locals in the United States and Canada. The New York, Los Angeles, and Toronto locals have memberships running in the thousands, whereas locals such as Newport News, Virginia, or Fitchburg, Massachusetts, have fewer than two hundred members each. Most of the locals received their AFM charters some years ago, when it took a sizable amount of time to travel distances of fifty or seventy-five miles. For example, Colorado, which has a population under three million, has separate AFM locals in Boulder, Colorado Springs, Denver, Grand Junction, Greeley, and Pueblo. Denver and Boulder are only twenty-five miles apart, but each local has a territorial jurisdiction. In areas of low population density, a local may control a territory of hundreds of square miles.

The working conditions, population base, and problems of each local may vary considerably. In New York, Los Angeles, Nashville, and Toronto, there is a great deal of recording work for commercials, movies, television shows, and phonograph records. Comparatively little of this work is done elsewhere, although Chicago does a respectable number of commercials, and there are a number of high-quality recording studios in Miami and in Muscle Shoals, Alabama. Other markets also pick up a certain amount of recording work. Naturally, the interests of the musicians who work in the large recording centers are quite different from the concerns of those who work the local clubs in small towns in Indiana or South Dakota. The International Executive Board of the AFM negotiates all recording contracts, and all scales (minimum wages) are set nationally, with a few exceptions that will be discussed later. The various union locals set the scales for the nightclubs, concert halls, and theaters in their territories.

To understand the way the union operates today, it is useful to look at the way it has developed over the years. The predecessor of the AFM was the National League of Musicians, dating back to 1885. Because the NLM considered the interests of musicians to be on a higher social level than those of laborers, the NLM turned down several invitations to affiliate with the American Federation of Labor (AFL). In 1896, the AFL chartered the American Federation of Musicians, and it quickly overcame the influence of the NLM.[1] Joseph Weber was the first strong president of the AFM, and he held this position from 1900 to 1940.

During the years of Weber's presidency, the working conditions of musicians underwent drastic changes. Some thirty-five thousand musicians were employed through the 1920s in movie theaters, playing for silent movies. After the arrival of talking pictures in 1927, these musicians quickly lost their jobs. Other losses of employment were caused by the passing of the legitimate road show and the gradual phasing out of vaudeville. Radio became an important source of work for musicians, employing 2,237 musicians in 1940. However, that same year the Supreme Court ruled that it was permissible for radio stations to play records.[2] Stations cut down on the size of their orchestras and eventually eliminated virtually all live music.

In the same year, James Caesar Petrillo became president of the AFM, and he decided to combat the unemployment of musicians, which he attributed to the wide use of phonograph records. In 1942, Petrillo called a strike against the record companies that lasted for twenty-seven months. During this time the union would not allow musicians to make phonograph records. At first, the record companies released recordings that they had stockpiled against the eventuality of a strike; later, vocal groups were used to imitate with their voices the sounds of musical instruments. Because the union did not admit ocarina or harmonica players, some records were made with those instruments. For the most part, the strike was successful in crippling the record industry, and Decca Records was the first major company to sign a new agreement, in September 1943. Decca then started to sign some of the RCA and Columbia artists who were still unable to record.

In November 1944, RCA and Columbia signed agreements with the union. These new agreements set up the Recording and Transcription Fund, which was later reorganized as the Music Performance Trust Fund (MPTF). This fund remains active today. All record companies that sign agreements with the AFM pledge to contribute a percentage of their gross profits to the MPTF. The MPTF trustee is appointed by the record companies and must be approved by the Secretary of Labor. This trustee approves all MPTF contracts. The contracts provide for free performances of live music at veterans' hospitals, schools, and nursing homes. Many of these performances are entirely funded by the MPTF, but some utilize matching funds from commercial sponsors such as banks to provide live music at shopping malls or in city parks. No admission may be charged to MPTF performances.

Petrillo felt that the MPTF provided a hedge against unemployment of musicians through the use of phonograph records. His next move was to attempt the extension of the MPTF concept to movies, television, and commercials. Eventually the musicians who worked in those fields rebelled against Petrillo, because they came to believe that he was willing to sacrifice wage increases for these studio musicians in favor of greater amounts of money for the MPTF funds. The Los Angeles local was the center of this dissatisfaction. This disagreement became so acute that some studio musicians defected and formed their own union, the Musicians' Guild.[3] The guild operated from 1958 to 1961. During those years, it defeated the AFM in an election for jurisdiction over the movie industry and also gained control over a small portion of the phonograph record industry. Just before the formation of the guild, four lawsuits were filed against the AFM by members of the Los Angeles local, seeking to recover monies paid into the MPTF. These suits claimed that Petrillo had traded wage increases for studio musicians for increased MPTF payments and sought retroactive payment for studio musicians and an end to the MPTF funds.

In 1958, Petrillo decided not to seek reelection, and Herman Kenin, the new president, proved more conciliatory toward the interests of the studio musicians. The suits were all settled, and it was agreed that the MPTF would stay intact for phonograph records. Half the money would be paid into the Special Payments Fund. That money is returned to the musicians who play on records at the end of each year, based on the amount of their scale wages during that year. The MPTF was phased out of recording sessions that involve television, movie work, or commercials. For these media it no longer exists. The money in the Special Payments Fund is considerable; for the year 1980, the payments exceeded $18 million.[4]

Petrillo felt that the studio musicians were the fat cats of the musicians' union; by creating the MPTF, he intended to provide work for unemployed musicians. There is no question that the MPTF results in the presentation of live music in many places that would not otherwise employ musicians, but one could argue that the fund more commonly provides extra work for musicians who are already employed. The resolution of the MPTF controversies was of prime importance to the future of the union, because Petrillo's actions had created a split in the membership not unlike the friction between unskilled and skilled workers in industrial unions like the United Automobile Workers (UAW).

At the present time, there are some issues in the recording industry that could prove as volatile as the MPTF crisis. Because the recording scales are set nationally, they generally reflect the standards of the musicians who work in the New York, Los Angeles, and Nashville locals, where the bulk of the recording is done. The 1982 union minimum wage for phonograph records is over $150 for a three-hour recording session. For radio and television commercials, the wage is $64.40 an hour plus reuse payments (called residuals) every thirteen weeks. Given the overall budgets of the large record companies and the producers of network commercials, these are reasonable sums. The problem is that in the smaller markets, records are often pressed in small quantities, and commercials are made for local products that have low budgets. It is not unusual for local performers in the smaller markets to form their own record companies and to press five hundred to a thousand copies of their records. For commercials, there is a category called local commercials for those which are recorded in one union local and used in that local's territory. In this circumstance, the scale is 50 percent of national scale. If the commercial is used in the territory of two locals, it is classified as a national commercial. In other words, if I record a commercial in Denver that is aired in Denver and Boulder, this is regarded by the union as a national commercial, just as though it were airing on national television. Keep in mind that Boulder is twenty-five miles from Denver, and you can see how absurd this situation is in the 1980s. The 1982–3 AFM jingle contract does include some provisions for regional buy-outs. In my opinion the contract is still a bit unrealistic, but at least it represents a step in the right direction.

Many union members simply ignore these rules. Musicians in small and medium-size markets who are union members do in fact play on recording sessions for local commercials, recordings, and low-budget industrial films for less than union scale, and this without union contracts. The union that has jurisdiction over singers, the American Federation of Radio and Television Artists (AFTRA), has more sophisticated recording agreements for commercials which utilize the concepts of local and regional scales. Each category uses different minimum payments, and buy-outs

of commercials providing for lengthy uses without additional payments are permitted. AFTRA also has a bonus system for those
who sing background parts on records that become best sellers.
This system provides for bonus payments at various sales pla-
teaus. The 1981 AFM commercials agreement has instituted
some provisions for one-year buy-outs and regional uses, but the
scales are still very unrealistic by the standards of smaller markets.
When union members play on recording sessions without contracts, they must verbally negotiate their wages, and they are not
protected by union contracts. The union loses out by receiving
no work dues on those jobs. It is impossible to estimate the extent
of nonunion recording, but in the Denver area, a medium-sized
market, there are at least a half dozen companies that make
commercials as a full-time occupation. None of them are sig-
natories to the union agreements.

At the low end of the recording picture, the AFM needs to
recognize that budgets determine wages. In smaller markets the
budgets often cannot justify high pay scales. Record companies
could pay musicians according to the number of records manufactured, with bonuses paid on new pressings. This would be
difficult to monitor, but it is clearly better than ignoring the situation entirely. Commercials should be scaled according to the
AFTRA system, with a recognition of population differences. Similarly, film scores should be scaled according to budgets. This is
done to some extent with feature films, but I am referring to local
industrial or promotional films. This sort of work is done all over
North America, and a good deal of it is done nonunion.

If the union fails to institute these reforms, members will continue to work unprotected and in violation of their union oath.
To produce a truly equitable system will require a great deal of
thought on the part of the International Executive Board, small
record companies, film companies, and producers of commercials. The union must also eventually differentiate between radio
and television commercials. Currently, these commercials pay
identical wages, although the budgets of television commercials
are gigantic in comparison to those of radio commercials. Re-

cording musicians ought to share in the large monies budgeted for filming and time buys of television commercials; also, the scales for radio commercials should perhaps be lower than they are at present. Basic to the current recording scales is the assumption that all the work is done in the major recording centers. In fact, recording hardware has proliferated in all parts of North America. There are numerous multitrack recording studios in such cities as Denver, Seattle, and Omaha.

The problem with changing recording scales to reflect contemporary conditions is that it is difficult to reprogram advertisers, record companies, or the union when these people have been negotiating the current agreements for some years. What is necessary, is a reevaluation of the entire recording process and its financing in the 1980s. This is a difficult process but one that is absolutely necessary in order to reflect the conditions of our day.

In the last five years, the AFM has experienced a decline in membership. In 1976, there were 331,672 members; in 1978, 326,544; in 1979, 306,976; and in 1980, 291,281.[5] At the 1981 convention in Salt Lake City in June, the 1981 membership was estimated at about 280,000. There are several reasons for this loss of membership. The state of the music business has not been particularly good. The record business has experienced a slowdown of its phenomenal growth of the 1970s. From around 1977 to 1980, disco music achieved great popularity, and many nightclubs that formerly employed musicians turned to a policy of hiring disc jockeys to spin the latest disco hits. This situation became so serious that a number of locals picketed nightclubs that use the disco format.

Several internal matters in the union structure have also resulted in loss of membership. Most union locals are set up to serve the big band musician and the symphony player. This is partly a matter of stability; these groups are easy to locate because they have definite schedules set up in advance. Thus it takes a minimum of policing to collect the union taxes, called work dues, that working members pay. The work dues structure varies widely from local to local. It can be as little as ½ of one percent of scale wages to as much as 5 percent in some locals. At the AFM convention in 1980, the federation passed a uniform 1 percent work dues, half of which goes to the national office and half to the local. This was the first uniform work dues levied on all members, and many locals resisted it. It was necessary because the federation incurred a deficit of $912,640 in 1979.[6] Some locals had not previously required work dues, and in these locals members did not have to file contracts with the union. Thus, there was no written record of these jobs, and some members probably used this as a way of not bothering to report such income when filing tax returns. Under the new work dues system, there is a written record of all jobs. The larger locals had all used a system of work dues for some time, and so this was not an issue for them. At the 1981 convention, numerous resolutions were proposed calling for repeal of the work tax, but the national leadership lobbied heavily to retain it. On a roll call vote, the national leadership was victorious; the union voted 232,038 to 46,518 to retain the work dues. This vote occurred despite the contention of a number of locals that they had lost membership because of the work dues.

I mentioned that the union is set up to service the band musician. In contrast, the country and western or rock musicians who usually perform in self-contained musical groups of three to five musicians feel that they are not really a part of the union structure. At the 1981 national convention, music preceded and followed each business session. The music was invariably swing-oriented jazz music. The people in the band that did most of the playing varied in age from forty-five to sixty years. No country and western, rock and roll, rhythm and blues, or folk music was played. In most locals of the union, the same situation prevails. The symphony and big band musicians do not really consider the younger members who play other styles of music to be true professional musicians. It is probably true, although difficult to prove, that most of the union's local and international leadership feels a certain contempt for today's music. The typical nightclub job or college concert is performed by a small band that seldom includes these older musicians.

There is a gap between the union leadership and the typical working musician. This gap is a broad one and it includes differences of age, dress, and general interest. On a more formal musical level, many of the pop musicians of today do not read music, or they use written music as an insignificant part of their working life. Most band or symphony musicians cannot play without written music. This indicates major differences in training, orientation, and musical preference. It is as difficult for the union leadership to understand this difference as it is for the music educator. The philistines are invading formerly sacred territory, and the territory is proving indefensible because of the nature of such differences between teenagers and middle-aged adults. When I attended the 1981 convention as an elected delegate from the Denver local, I, at forty-six, appeared to be one of the younger delegates.

There are other reasons why the contemporary musician is alienated from the union. Forty or fifty years ago, the average American worker became unionized, but since that time many Americans have come to view unions as another layer of bureaucracy to be placed on top of the already overladen structure of state, local, and national government, of corporations and conglomerates of all sizes and descriptions. The first question that the young musician asks is usually, "What does the union do for me?" It is a common mistake among young people to think that unions get work for people. In fact many unions expend considerable energy protecting people who already have work against competition from younger people. In the New York local of the AFM, when you join the union, you must sign a statement that you are not joining to get a job that was promised to you. On the other hand, you may not join the Screen Actors' Guild (SAG) until you have a written promise of employment. Other talent unions restrict the number of new members through high initiation fees or dues. The intent of the Local 802 restriction is to keep musicians from taking jobs from the existing membership, and the idea of the SAG rule is to discourage people from entering the film business on faith alone.

Actually, it is possible to get some work through the Musicians' Union. Some locals keep availability lists. These are forms that indicate what instruments a musician plays; whether he or she reads, improvises, or sings; whether he or she is willing to travel; and what style of music he or she plays. The names are referred to prospective employers or other musicians looking for new personnel. In the Denver local, a book is kept that is open to any member for inspection, listing all requests for musicians that come to the union. These jobs include wedding receptions, dances, and concerts. In other locals, such as New York, there are so many members and the staff of the union itself is so large that there is no formal referral system. However, on Monday, Wednesday, and Friday afternoons, the New York musicians gather in the basement ballroom and exchange referrals and news of casual jobs.

Although the union does not guarantee work for its members, it does offer a variety of useful services. The International Executive Board negotiates all national contracts. In addition to recording, this includes touring shows such as the Ice Follies and the circus. On all these contracts, there are pension and welfare payments made for each musician. The local unions negotiate minimums for clubs, theaters, or concert halls. Thanks to these negotiations, the individual member is relieved of the responsibility of having to bargain for wages on each job. Since most recording sessions are booked with twelve to twenty-four hours' notice, such bargaining would be extremely difficult. The union only sets minimum wages, and some of the top players have been able to demand over-scale payments for their services.

Other benefits of membership are contingent upon the size of the local. Typical benefits include discounts on merchandise, low-interest loans from credit unions, and participation in medical plans. In the smaller locals, the benefits are necessarily minimal. The AFM sponsors an annual Congress of Strings for young string players, and some locals have workshops in reading music.

The New York local also sponsors a Senior Orchestra for retired members that plays symphonic music in concerts.

I would like to see a series of educational programs that could include seminars on the music business, songwriting workshops, and seminars on legal protection for musicians. In many locals there are experienced members who could be helpful in the presentation of such programs. The national union is planning to institute a toll-free telephone line that will enable members to get job listings in various parts of the country. This will be a useful service to members who are interested in traveling bands. There are some private organizations that have such referral services, but they charge for it and have no interest in whether their buyers are protected by union contracts. It might also serve a variety of purposes if the union would promote workshops in contemporary musical styles in which some of the younger members could demonstrate their skills to the older players. This might include such subjects as electronic music, contemporary musical styles, and modern songwriting.

One of the most serious crises in the union is the loss of traveling members, the musicians who play in various jurisdictions. Under AFM rules, these members used to have to pay 10 percent of their scale wages when working steady jobs in a local in which they did not hold membership. A steady job is one of three days or longer. To reduce what was clearly an exorbitant and punitive tax the union has changed this rule so that the travelling musician now pays the same work tax that the members of the local in whose territory he is playing must pay. This tax varies from .005 to 4.5 percent of scale. This is a much better system, but because the travelling member is rarely in one place for very long, he has little chance to utilize the services of the union, and often feels out of touch with it. If he gets into a contractual dispute with an employer, he often must go to another town to work rather than wait around for the union to help file charges against the employer. Vincent Fuentealba, president of the AFM, recognizes this problem and has established a toll-free national telephone number to help resolve such difficulties. The federation has also taken on many of the legal costs that arise when travelling musicians get into disputes with their employers. Unfortunately, many of the motel chains that hire traveling musicians do not care whether they employ union members. This means that leaving the union does not necessarily make a traveling member less employable, as it would in the recording field.

Outmoded rules govern the transfer of membership from one local to another. When a musician moves from one city to another, he or she cannot accept a steady job working at a club. The musician must bring a union card to the office of the new local and deposit it there for three months. During this time the musician can work one-night engagements but not steady jobs. This rule is intended to discourage raiding, or the attempt to take steady jobs outside the musician's home local. The modern automobile and highway system and the social structure of North America have created a nation of people on the move. There is also no denying that there are many jobs available in the thriving population areas of the southwestern Sunbelt. The musician often keeps his or her old membership and adds membership in the new local as well. About twenty-three thousand members of the AFM hold membership in more than one local.[7] In some cases a musician may belong to as many as three or four locals, paying dues to each one.

I have said very little about the way in which the union represents symphony players. These musicians have their own organization, the International Conference of Symphony & Opera Musicians (ICSOM). Contracts are negotiated locally in each jurisdiction. Some legal support is provided through the union locals, although in some instances the musicians prefer to select and pay their own attorneys. The problems that arise in the symphonic field are quite similar to the difficulties that occur between labor and management in a factory situation. Some of these disputes include working conditions, such as the type of stools that the cello section may prefer; procedures that govern asking for leave to audition for a better orchestra; the rotation of musical parts, especially in the string section to avoid boredom; and the relationships between the orchestra members, conductors, visiting conductors, and colleagues. Sometimes there is a difference of opinion between members of the orchestra and management over what constitutes acceptable behavior. One member of the Denver Symphony who hates popular music appeared at a "pops" concert wearing earmuffs and hiding behind his cello. This kind of behavior can lead to a grievance procedure on the part of the management or another member of the orchestra who may consider such an action as unprofessional behavior.

The AFM is a difficult organization to administer because of the large number of locals. Some consolidation of these locals would make the union easier to run and would also help to centralize costs, such as the salaries of local officers. This consolidation process is happening gradually as a result of attrition, but it would make more sense for the various locals and the international union to encourage it actively. Lately it seems to be doing so.

The union has been fighting hard to achieve a performance right for its members when records are played on the radio. If this were enacted, radio stations would pay a small royalty for the right to play records. This royalty would be split up among the musicians, the singers, the artist who made the record, and the recording companies. In Europe performance rights already exist, although the nature of the split varies among countries. It seems inevitable that some sort of performance royalty will eventually be granted, because the only ones opposed to it are the radio station owners and managers.

In the Pacific Northwest, the AFM was forced to go into the booking-agency business because the agents refused to cooperate with the union. The union created its own agency, Music Central, operated by the Puget Sound Council of Locals. It operates in Alaska, Montana, Idaho, Oregon, Washington, and southwest Canada. So far Music Central has achieved some success in its work, but the problem with union-sponsored booking agencies in other areas is that they might cut into territories served by union-licensed agents. In such circumstances one could expect these agents to abandon their union franchises. This could be a potentially dangerous situation, but it will be interesting to see whether Music Central grows or the union tries to spread it to other geographic locations. The Bakersfield, California, local actually runs a nightclub featuring live music, and the Denver local is contemplating a similar step. With such a facility, the union can feature live music regularly, and of course it can also make sure that it hires only union musicians for the available jobs.

If the Musicians' Union is to survive the 1980s, it must begin to concentrate on providing services to its younger members. It would be nice to see a national convention of the union featuring many styles of music and many age groups. At the 1981 convention, the Los Angeles local proposed that the union consider some sort of confederation or amalgamation with the existing talent unions, especially AFTRA and SAG. Whether such a confederation evolved into a literal amalgamation or only into some joint projects, it would give the union more muscle, particularly in national recording agreements, where the musicians and singers do not always work closely together. At present the International Executive Board of the AFM is considering this proposal. Sooner or later the union must work to revise existing recording scales so that they reflect conditions in all parts of North America, not only the major cities.

The union needs to broaden its concept of educational functions and to encourage its members in a truly creative dialogue about the business aspects of music and the aesthetics of musical style. Something must be done to limit the financial responsibilities of the traveling members and to provide them with more services. To make up for the resulting loss of income, the union should consider putting a surcharge on work dues when the performers are earning way above scale. The top recording groups rarely play for longer than one night in a single location, and so they seldom pay the traveling tax. For example, when a group like the Eagles plays an auditorium concert and comes away with $25,000, their work dues are still based on the union minimum wage, as though they were a local dance combo. If the work dues are 2.5 percent and the scale is $50 per musician with double for the leader, these work dues would be 2.5 percent of $300, or a total of $7.50. At this rate it is hardly worthwhile to do the paperwork. A progressive tax that takes actual wages into account could bring much-needed money into the union treasury, provided that the union could explain to the rock and country stars why this money is necessary and why they should pay their fair share. Even if the one-night work dues were doubled, the cost to the traveling artists would be minimal, considering how much money they are paid for a night's work.

There are currently no women, black, or Hispanic musicians holding positions on the union's executive board. This lack of representation certainly does not indicate the considerable contributions of these groups to the union or to music in general. The board is elected at the national convention by the delegates so that minority representation can be achieved only if the delegates themselves spend time thinking about the fact that the board does not represent minority groups or younger musicians. The bottom line is that the union needs to organize the unorganized younger musicians and that this membership in turn needs to participate in union affairs by going to meetings and electing officers and convention delegates to represent their interests.

As we move into a more advanced electronic age, there will be more and more electronic musical instruments, cable television hookups, and video discs. The most practical approach is not to resist these devices, as Petrillo did in the past, but to work with the new technology. It is of prime importance to the future of the AFM that the leadership be a dynamic group of people dedicated to the music and musicians of the future. We should not ignore the music of the past, and we cannot ignore the music of the future.

THE ARTIST AND THE
AUDIENCE

The artist in America is a lonely individual leading a life that is generally far removed from the "important" activities of society. The intellectual focus is on the scientist, and scientific or pseudoscientific thought dominates philosophy and the physical and social sciences. Hard science receives the heaviest monetary support for research projects, whereas the arts scramble for their relatively small slice of governmental funding. Modern technology dominates our lives, taking precedence over humanistic values and artistic processes. We teach our children to use rational and objective methods as the preferred way of viewing reality.

On a more pragmatic level, we seek to acquire as many possessions and as much money as we can. This drive is tempered by a perpetual quest for security. We want an early and lengthy retirement period, a sort of eternal vacation. These material goals provide the context for the working lives of most Americans.

Art is not a scientific process, nor does it provide financial rewards or security for the great majority of its practitioners. Because art is essentially a subjective process, it cannot be viewed in the rational and objective manner in which we consider a field like computer programming. The very conditions that produce art and under which artists work seem antithetical to the values of American society and may bring the artist into conflict with the social structure.

The consumer, the person who purchases a work of art or a ticket to a performance, tends to view art as a service industry. The artist is seen as one who serves the purchaser of art. For the artist, art is a central preoccupation, not an auxiliary activity. This conflict creates a seemingly unbridgeable gap between the way the creative person views his or her work and the way the audience sees it. Many of the misunderstandings between the artist and the audience relate to this fundamental difference of opinion. The artist approaches his or her work with commitment and seriousness, but the consumer views it as a piece of entertainment. No one needs a painting in the same sense that he or she needs to see a doctor or have a car inspected. Art is a pleasant accessory but still a luxury item to a culture whose orientation is practical and businesslike.

The difference in attitude between the artist and the audience leads to a fundamental misunderstanding between the two parties. We often hear people say, "I want to be entertained when I read a novel. I don't want to deal with anything heavy; there's enough of that in my work and my life." Consider how this viewpoint restricts creativity. An artist is a person who has devoted a lifetime to the development of skills in the same fashion as a doctor or an educator. Yet we seem to view the artist as an entertainer or minstrel. In contrast, we see the doctor or auto mechanic as a skilled professional with a high degree of commitment and expertise. It is ridiculous to dictate what the artist can do and to proscribe whole areas of thought or feeling as being unacceptable because the consumer may not like them. Limiting the artist to telling an audience what it wants to hear is tantamount to censorship.

Because the artist requires an audience and has the same desire for financial success and ego gratification as anyone else, we have experienced the phenomenon of "popular culture." If I am compelled to distinguish between popular and serious art, I would use as my criterion the seriousness of the artist's intentions, insofar as this can be determined. The later music of the Beatles may have achieved mass popularity, but I consider it serious music. I could cite numerous examples of classical music composers or performers whose work I would categorize as being in the domain of popular culture. Perhaps the last word on this subject belongs to my friend Wes Westbrooks, whom you have already met in the chapter on "Music as a Part-Time Profession." At a party that Wes attended, a concert pianist asked if he wrote or performed "serious" music. Wes was at a loss to reply, but several days later he said to me, "I've never known a musician who isn't serious about his music."

How did such a barrier between the artist and the audience come into being? If we look at the role of the artist in primitive society, we find that there is no such removal of art from the life of the average person. Dancing, singing, and crafts are part of the everyday life of the tribe, and all are expected to participate. In Bali there is no separate word for art, because the artist is not considered to be isolated from the life of the community.[1] Imagine telling a typical American blue-collar worker that he or she is expected to participate in a three-day ritual celebrating the coming of spring. Such an announcement would probably result in the announcer becoming an involuntary patient at the local mental hospital.

However, we must concede that innovation is not encouraged in primitive art. Radically new methods are not apt to be encouraged by the society or attempted by the artist. There must be a good deal of innovative primitive art that is nipped in the bud because the society has no context in which to place it. Perhaps integrated social structures are achieved at the cost of conformity to the society.

The communication of art in our society usually involves some sort of frustrating interaction between the creator and the consumer. The painter has work displayed in an art gallery or museum alongside other, often unrelated works of art. These restrictions do not apply to the superstar Picassos of the world, who can determine the conditions of their exhibitions or who don't even have to do so because the people running the displays would not dream of insulting them. Consider the conditions under which the "opening" of the exhibition occurs. There are the wine-sipping socialites and the precious dilettantes who attend the opening, and there is a particular sort of ambience and conversational atmosphere that is part of the social world of the gallery or art museum. None of this has anything to do with the art itself, but it has a great deal to do with the sort of reception or acceptance that the work of the artist will receive. If no one comes to the opening, there will be no newspaper or magazine articles and no reviews, and none of the paintings will be sold.

In classical music, we are confronted by the sterile atmosphere of the concert hall, with its well-dressed, starched, and polite customers. Some of them are in attendance in order to display the latest in clothes or coiffures and some to display their charitable support of the arts; some come because a close relative has insisted upon it, and a few even come to listen to the music! I have always been fascinated when a slow or complex piece of music is performed and the audience feels compelled to cough, as though they were making some feeble attempt to participate in what Murray Schafer calls the soundscape.[2] I suppose they are participating by expressing their discomfort at having to listen to a piece of unpleasant or incomprehensible music.

Consider the jazz musician, playing in a nightclub which functions as a sort of mating environment for its patrons. The club usually sells alcohol, and the patrons view the scene as an opportunity to get drunk, dance, snap their fingers, or make or enhance their contacts with members of the opposite sex. There is nothing intrinsically wrong with pursuing these activities, but the atmosphere generated by such an audience does little to inspire a musician to the imaginative flights of improvisation that the audience supposedly came to witness. The musicians are more than aware that most of the audience is not paying close attention to the music. In many clubs it is not possible to listen closely because the background noise of the cash register and the bar rivals the volume level of the music. I remember seeing the great jazz saxophone player John Coltrane performing at the Village Gate in New York in 1965. At two o'clock in the morning, there were twenty or thirty people left in a club that holds several hundred. The lightman blinked the lights over and over in an attempt to signal Coltrane that it was time to close. Coltrane was in the middle of a long and complex improvisation, and since he was playing with his eyes closed, he either did not see the signal or chose to ignore it. Whenever I think of the dilemma of the performing musician, I remember that night.

A contemporary rock concert is a social event supreme, with thousands of raving, screaming teenagers. Some of the audience have passed out in their seats from the effects of alcohol or drugs. Clothes and hair styles create a kaleidoscope of colors to rival a light show. The whole event is more like a crazed movie set than a concert presentation. Despite a huge and powerful sound system, it is often difficult to hear anything over the noise of the crowd. This noise level may even make it difficult for the performers to hear one another or to keep their instruments in tune. Some rock groups add to the atmosphere of carnival madness by destroying musical instruments or doing provocative choreography. This sort of production brings us full circle to the participation of the tribe in the ritual, except that in the rock concert, the ritual is manipulative and is based upon the performer's ability to predict the behavior of the audience.

The performance of folk music before an audience presents some interesting problems, because folk music is traditionally more of a participatory experience than a performing one. When folk music is performed on a stage, it is removed from the living and breathing tradition that is organic to the music. In these circumstances, a performance can degenerate into a show business ritual, or it may be treated with such excessive seriousness that it is no longer enjoyable.

Even if an audience is quiet and respectful, we cannot compel it to think about the event itself. In fact, the listeners may be thinking about the latest office crisis or the cute lady in the adjacent row; in the case of a gallery opening, they may be there to taste the wine and eat the food. A scholarly friend of mine used to tell me that the Museum of Modern Art in New York was a great place to meet women.

It is difficult to involve the modern audience in the artistic event they have come to see. There are too many distractions, too many accompanying rituals that have nothing to do with the art itself.

The artist has personal goals or desires. Some of these objectives may be ego goals directed toward achieving status, recognition, fame, or economic success. That set of goals may be compatible with some of the goals of the audience. The consumer wishes to be recognized as a supporter of the arts who has good taste and keeps up with the latest trends. The artist may have a long list of more serious goals such as a wish to transcend the old modes of art in order to develop new insights. If the audience wishes only to be entertained, they may resist feeling anything very deeply. They may be unable to transcend their preexisting notions about an art form or the way the artist should use that art form.

Another artistic goal is to indoctrinate or educate the audience toward a particular social or political viewpoint. Marxists view art as a vehicle for moving the average person in the direction of Marxism. As the artist manipulates the proper symbols, the audience will feel appropriate sympathy or antagonism. In the Communist world, the audience is supposed to emerge from an artistic experience with their feelings about the validity of the state reinforced. This description of Marxist goals is obviously simplistic, but the fact is that in the Communist world, art is the obedient servant of the state. Such political assumptions constitute a severe limitation on the scope of the artist, although a great artist can overcome any limitations, assuming that the state-controlled media allow the artist's paintings to be shown, his novels to be published, or her symphony to be performed. The difference between the communist and capitalist view of art is the difference between control by the state and our more subtle control by the distribution mechanism that merchandises art. No one in the

United States forbids you to write a book or paint a painting, but there are no guarantees that your book will be published or your paintings exhibited. In the Communist world, any overt criticism of the state is a virtual guarantee that a work of art will not be permitted to circulate except in an illegal form that is not available to the public.

Any art that seeks to blaze new trails is bound to face some resistance.[3] There is a tendency on the part of the avant-garde to support new art for the sake of novelty or innovation. This places the avant-garde into direct conflict with the passive consumer, who prefers works that are familiar and comfortable. We have to distinguish between the glorification of the new for the sake of novelty and the sense of risk that serious artists bring to their endeavors. Artists need to feel that they are breaking new ground in order to nurture and develop their work. If the audience enjoyed an artist's earlier work, they may be upset by any radical changes in that artist's style. It is the same fluidity that makes art exciting that unfortunately also makes it confusing.

If an avant-garde posture represents a shallow approach by a particular artist, that artist may cultivate a high degree of cynicism and may wish to promote the view that the consumer will not understand the work of art anyway. This sort of ideology has led to absurd if colorful excesses in many contemporary art forms. The germ of truth found in the avant-garde view is that it is often true that the audience does not want to make the effort to understand anything new. If art is seen as entertainment and not as a serious pursuit, why should the audience want to be stretched, or colloquially speaking, bent out of shape, in pursuit of some complex idea or form?

Much of the difficulty between the artist and society stems from the way art is taught in the schools. We have discussed some of these problems in the chapter on music education. Suffice it to say that if art is presumed to be inferior to science, and if art is so complex that it can be produced only by experts, why should the average person attempt to exercise his or her intellect or emotions to comprehend something that he or she probably will not be able to grasp even with the necessary effort?

Another conflict between the artist and the audience results from the average person's conception that art is supposed to be beautiful. The artist's view of beauty may include such elements as ugliness, contrast, and horror. For the average person, these are not the characteristics of beauty.

Some consumers find themselves in a comparable role to that of the avant-garde artist. This sort of person wants to participate in an artistic experience that is beyond the reach of the average person.[4] This experience may be realized by purchasing an expensive piece of art or acquiring an unusual or rare work. On a more basic level, we find the culture vulture who always sees the new plays, reads the latest books, goes to openings at art galleries, or sees the new foreign films. This individual searches far and wide to find a favorite critic who confirms the value of a particular work of art. A conversation with one of these trendy types is often a monologue, because most of us (including artists) do not have the time or energy to follow every artistic trend. There are more consumers of this type in New York and Los Angeles than in other cities, because the latest in art is easily accessible there. In the smaller cities, no one knows or cares what these people are talking about.

The genuine visionary artist will take the viewer or listener on a trip beyond literal physical reality. The audience may resist this voyage because the destination is unclear. In other words, people tend to be uncomfortable when dealing with ambiguity. A whole other part of the art audience enjoys strange and mystical experiences because it is the irrational and the unknown that constitute reality for them. The popularity of astrology and any number of psychological self-help and therapeutic measures testifies to the size of this group. What our society seems to lack is well-integrated and rational people who remain open to emotional experiences and approach the unknown with interest rather than fear. After all, who can say with certainty that mystical concepts are invalid? It was not so long ago that doctors prescribed bloodletting as a cure for many diseases.

Art is vitally involved with the process of change.[5] The change may be a technical shift in the artist's style or an internal one in the mind or heart of the audience. If the audience is seeking escape, relaxation, or entertainment, change is the last thing it desires. There may be an additional element of discomfort if the audience senses that the artist is trying to initiate some sort of change in them. The artist may be presenting a new way of seeing, hearing, or experiencing something, or he or she may be orchestrating a campaign to influence the audience's social or political views. This advocacy of change may coincide with the artist's world view,[6] but the consumer may not wish to be reminded of controversial issues. It is not always possible to find an acceptable compromise between the two goals.

The artist has trouble understanding why the consumer is not willing to devote more time and energy to understanding works of art. The art consumer doesn't see why the artist cannot relate a message in a clear and simple manner. Given these differences in orientation, training, and concentration, coupled with contrasting levels of emotional commitment, it is no wonder that many artists develop a feeling of contempt or hostility for their public or that the audience wonders what it is that an artist is trying to say and why the artist has so much trouble expressing himself.

When we add to this complex stew the unpredictable nature of many artists, their frequently nonconformist life-styles, and the variety of goals that an artist may have even in a single work of art, it is no wonder that the average person finds the whole process confusing. The audience may wish to have their normal life patterns reinforced, but the artist is more concerned with illuminating the deeper and less rational aspects of life. The nature of reality carries different meanings for the two parties in this transaction.

The critic attempts to fill this void of understanding between the artist and the audience, making sense out of the artistic process and telling us what constitutes good work. We assume that the critic has the necessary background and experience to make these judgments. Still, the question arises as to why an average person cannot judge a work of art without some outside form of validation from an "expert." The good critic can serve as a tour guide, directing the audience's attention to what is most important and providing a context to help illuminate what may at first appear ambiguous. Tom Wolfe, in *The Painted Word*,[7] points out that in some cases the difficulty and complexity of the critic's evaluation of a work of art may far exceed the problems of understanding the work itself. In other words, the critic's exposition that was supposedly intended to clarify the work is in fact more complicated than the work itself. The critic is on dangerous ground when making assumptions about the artist's state of mind or when speculating about the artist's goals. A new work of art cannot always be explained or clarified through an initial contact. It takes time, sometimes a long time, before a piece of art can be absorbed into the audience's or critic's overall context. Until then, it is difficult to evaluate the work.

This is not intended to be an essay on the role of the critic, but perhaps we should ask some brief questions about the function of criticism. What the critic can do best is provide a context for us to use in interpreting a particular work of art. Rather than trying to sell us on individual judgments, the critic should leave us with the space in which to decide for ourselves. For example, what is a "good tone" on a musical instrument? Andrès Segovia may represent one aspect of tonal quality. If we are listening to a jazz guitarist, the criteria used to judge the tone would change entirely, as they would in listening to a folk or blues player. It is an unfortunate mistake for a critic to judge a very specific art form by the standards that apply to another medium. Someone who is knowledgeable about Schoenberg's system of composition is not necessarily a good judge of bebop improvisation. In fact, most people who are highly aware of specific aspects of music or dance performance, for example, have a less than adequate knowledge of other media, even in the same art form. Critics may also betray a tendency to generalize from one specific art experience to another in a way that is not supported by the facts and that betrays their own cultural bias or training. It is rare for critics to admit that they do not understand a work of art or are not sure what to think about it. If critics would allow themselves this sort of flexibility and possibility for error, perhaps the audience would be able to accept uncertainty as a valid aspect of an art experience.

Sometimes the artist falls into the trap of trying to explain a piece of art by giving it a title that is intended to explain the meaning of the work. This may make sense, as in Debussy's *La Mer,* but often the artist is displaying a cynical view of the audience's ability to relate to a work. The artist must allow the listener or viewer some space in which to interpolate his or her feelings into the artistic experience. Part of this space also belongs to the artist, in the sense that he or she should be allowed room for failure. A piece of music may not come off in the way that the composer intended, despite the fact that it received a good performance. The nature of growth requires the possibility of failure and the use of that experience by the artist for further development and growth.

The patrons of art, the people who contribute heavily to the symphony orchestra or the art museum, often have a class bias that discourages experimentation and favors art that is traditional and unthreatening. Obviously, most of the art of the present era will not survive our time, just as the bulk of paintings, plays, and music from the past have been forgotten. However, if the modern orchestra does not perform any contemporary music, as is the case with most American orchestras, there is virtually no chance that these works will survive, and there is little motivation for the young composer to continue working. Most arts organizations are all too responsive to the wishes of their financial benefactors, and these patrons tend to be conservative in their artistic orientation. This is discouraging to the young and experimental artist.

The artist is constantly working on his or her art and questioning its value. This sort of obsession doesn't fit comfortably into forty-hour work weeks or make for easy or relaxed life-styles, nor does it follow the typical pattern of American family life. Artists are notorious for forming and breaking intense personal relationships and for multiple marriages and divorces. Additional tensions are created by the fact that most artists do not reap the kind of healthy financial reward that their commitment of time and energy would seem to deserve. It may be difficult for the artist to justify the amount of time spent on his or her working life to a spouse who is trying to balance the family budget. Moreover, success during one stage of an artist's life provides no assurance that the artist's earnings will continue to appreciate. Changing tastes can make an artist's particular skill obsolete with frightening rapidity. Thirty years ago, there were thousands of accordion players in America. Many of them worked as teachers, some performed in nightclubs, and a few became famous entertainers. In the last fifteen years, the accordion has virtually disappeared from the contemporary musical scene. One wonders what happened to those thousands of accordion players whose profession fell victim to changing tastes for no particular reason and through no fault of their own.

The development of modern technology has had a profound influence on some forms of art. The phonograph record influences what music is performed in public and is a complex medium in its own right. Today we see the peculiar phenomenon of popular musicians attempting to recreate in live performance effects that were achieved in a recording studio.[8] Apparently, what the bar audience wants to hear is a live and smiling version of the jukebox. The media of film and videotape have similarly made profound changes in the lives of actors. Why worry about memory lapses or mistakes when a retake of a scene will produce a level of mechanical perfection that is not available in the theater?

Artist and audience alike have been influenced by the role of changing technology. Records and videotapes form the sort of permanent record that we seem to enjoy in our society and that gives the artist some semblance of immortality. A contrasting view can be found in the culture of the Chopi musicians of Mozambique. These musicians compose suites of symphonic scope, some of them lasting as long as an hour. They are not written down, and once a performance has been completed, the composer and musicians cheerfully forget that work and go on to create new music. In Chopi society, it is the process of creation that is venerated. We focus our approval on the artifacts of art rather than on art itself. I am not saying that we should forsake the art of the past. I am suggesting that worshiping the art of past generations to the extent that we do changes our experience of art to an archeological one rather than a living and breathing experience that requires our attention and participation.

Composers or playwrights require conductors, performers, directors, or actors to present their work to the public. This introduces an additional variable between the originator of the work and the way in which the public experiences it. Moreover, conductors and actors are often better known than the composers or playwrights whose work is being performed so that the originator of the work may have little influence over its interpretation. In the recording industry, the record producer performs a similar function of control. In popular music, this process has gone so far that sometimes performers do not get to sing or play on records released under their own names. Such records are performed by professional studio musicians and singers, and the actual group learns the performances by listening to the records. Some of the letter-perfect performances on classical music records reflect considerable time spent in editing and splicing various versions of the same music. Such a performance can never be reproduced in person.

Many artists are able to work only part-time at their profession, and they rely on teaching jobs or unrelated work to provide economic security. These part-timers are often bitter about their lack of success, placing the blame on the audience. A young student who studies with such a teacher may develop the same contempt for the public. This process may be a subtle one, or the teacher may speak openly about his or her feelings.

Because art is packaged and sold like any other commodity, the sales of the product may often reflect skill in packaging more than the nature of the content. It is always easy to blame failure on the bad taste of the general public. My own view is that there is no strong correlation between artistic and commercial success, either positively or negatively. The unsuccessful artist has a number of alternatives. The artist may seek to find new ways of merchandising or may change the art itself to bring it into closer accord with what appears to appeal to the public. This is often referred to as "selling out." It is not always so easy to adopt existing styles, because a specific style may be closely identified with the work of a particular artist, and the public may resent another artist's attempts at imitation.

For the artist who is seeking an outlet but is not concerned with financial rewards, there are vanity records, vanity book publishers, and even art galleries that will rent space. Vanity products are paid for by the artist rather than by the publisher or record company. They are usually packaged in a way that makes them resemble commercial products, but they are manufactured in limited quantities and not distributed to the general public. The singer or writer purchases most of the copies of the work and sells them to friends or through local book or record stores. I see nothing wrong with the production of works of vanity art, unless the artist is duped into believing that they will be distributed in the marketplace like normal commercial products.

It is difficult to get a new and genuinely unique work of art to be accepted by the general public. When art is accepted and assimilated into the culture, the very qualities that made it original and challenging no longer disturb the audience.[9] Music that was shockingly atonal in 1920 now functions as background music for murder mysteries. Each innovative work of art goes through the stages of initial rejection by the audience, followed by endorsement by other artists or the critics, before it reaches broad acceptance. There will always be artists seeking new ways to express their visions. The unpredictable nature of art is one of its most exciting qualities.

Herbert Marcuse speaks of our culture's great capacity to absorb new cultural trends and turn them into commodities.[10] To put it another way, not everyone who listened to or liked Bob Dylan in 1963 necessarily understood the criticisms he was leveling at our society. They may have liked his hair or clothes or the sensual sound of his voice; they may never even have noticed the lyrics of his songs. It is probably true that only in American society could Bob Dylan become a millionaire by criticizing the society and life-styles of other millionaires.

I have not dwelled here on the differences between popular art and so-called high art forms. A lot of nonsense has been written about pop culture, and I am not sure that the distinctions between these forms are as real as many critics would have us believe. It is true that popular culture is cleverly and expensively merchandised, but there is a long tradition of pandering to the tastes of the public, going back through such august names as Paganini and Liszt. Paganini was a virtuoso violinist, and he was renowned for deliberately breaking three of the strings on his violin and proceeding to play melodies on the remaining string.[11] Liszt was able to virtually duplicate complete orchestral scores on the piano because of his technical wizardry. These are eighteenth- and nineteenth-century examples of showmanship, not of serious art.

The media coverage that has been extended to such superstars as Leonard Bernstein, Beverly Sills, and Luciano Pavarotti certainly rivals the attention given to pop music stars. Columbia has even marketed a series of classical records under such titles as *Mozart's Greatest Hits* in an attempt to cash in on standard pop music procedures. We seem to regard "high" culture as complex, serious, and worthy of respect. We think of pop culture as being on a low level of complexity but possessed of an extraordinary ability to generate sales.[12]

A curious example of how art can be simultaneously promoted and degraded and yet may endure is provided by the history of ragtime music. The grace and beauty of Scott Joplin's music gave rise to the Tin Pan Alley version of ragtime, in which the music was simplified and played at faster, happier tempos. The movie *The Sting* brought ragtime back to the popular music scene and helped to renew a serious interest in ragtime. This resulted in a

Broadway performance of Joplin's opera *Treemonisha*, something that had not occurred in the composer's lifetime.

Jazz is another kind of "popular" music that embraces a variety of styles in composition and performance. The use of improvisation embodies many of the artistic elements already discussed—risk, surprise, excitement, and anticipation. A truly improvised solo can never be performed twice in the same way.

There is something of a division in the jazz world between those who wish to play jazz according to their own vision of the music and those who wish to achieve commercial success by finding some musical formula that the public will buy. Only in recent years have jazz musicians actually strived to achieve significant commercial success. The noted sociologist Howard Becker makes a strong point about the way jazz musicians see themselves as outsiders in opposition to an audience of "squares."[13] As jazz-rock music has developed in the last five years or so, jazzmen have found their first vehicle for achieving success on the same terms as rock musicians. While purists are quick to charge that such musicians as Herbie Hancock or George Duke are selling out, it is up to the artist to decide what to do. It is as difficult to measure another person's integrity as it is to know what makes someone else happy.

It is an undeniable fact that much of popular art is disposable, whether it is in the form of movies, paintings, or songs. This trendiness further stimulates the merchandising apparatus of society to come up with new products. Although we may deplore the fickle nature of this process, the need for new art products is bound to create room for new artists. In this sense, we are in accord with the Chopi aesthetic of not hanging on to old art. Of course, we do write it all down, record it, or videotape it, and we have made societal nostalgia legitimate through golden-oldie records, silent movie festivals, and other modern tribal rituals. Our quest for permanence in art may be more of a sign of a refined embalming process than a verification of the value of a work of art. The fact that a particular piece of music continues to be performed after five hundred years is not necessarily an indication of its worth. Any number of factors may be responsible for a work remaining in circulation, including the personal taste of a conductor, a music publisher's efforts to promote a catalog, or simple accident.

We have seen that the goals of the artist and the audience are often at odds. There is a considerable lack of communication between the two groups, and there is very little understanding of art in contemporary American society. Rather than recapitulate the many points already discussed here, I will indicate some possible ways of improving the situation.

Our basic attitudes toward art are formed in the school and the family. When music and art are treated as serious yet entertaining subjects, perhaps children will be stimulated to devote as much attention to the arts as to algebra or social studies. Creative processes should be taught by encouraging children to create. Technique is of no value until the child has developed some interest in an art form. It is better to encourage children to write songs and then to discuss the shortcomings in their work than to ply them with details about the technical aspects of music.

It is time to remove art from the patronage basis which has historically been its main support in Western society. There should be music and art in our factories, in the schools, in the home, and on television. Every conceivable form of artistic expression should be represented so that no one will say, "I don't like art." State and local arts organizations should not necessarily focus on the support of existing major cultural institutions, such as symphony orchestras or art museums, but should expend more of their energies in persuading all cultural institutions and artists to relate to their audiences. There should be room in our society for social criticism, playfulness, beauty and ugliness, simplicity and complexity, experimentation and traditional approaches to art. Only when the artist and the audience can reach some sort of agreement can the arts flourish in a meaningful way. Until that time, art will be a specialized accessory utilized by the elite and misunderstood by the masses. Art should serve no master, but it should be aware of the needs of the people, even those needs which the people themselves do not recognize.

To create an environment that encourages the arts, we need the support of the schools, the government, and the media. The corporate world, the art world, and the various unions and guilds that represent artists need to acknowledge that not all art is financially self-sustaining, and some of it will never even reach the breakeven point. The media should not only sponsor artistic endeavors but also present discussions on the history of art, non-Western cultures, and in-depth portraits of artists. Public television has made some attempts in this direction, but it is handicapped by low budgets and a tendency to identify itself and artists in general as elite groups. We need to have more live music on radio and television. Some of it should be easy to understand and relate to, and some may require explanation and long-term exposure. In a reasonable society, all art can play an important role in enriching the lives of the people. Someday we can live in a world where the ordinary person and the artist can enrich each other's lives through shared experiences, goals, and insights. Such a society would also encourage the average person to paint, dance, act, write, play music, and think about the arts.

NOTES

INTRODUCTION

1. See Theodor W. Adorno, *Introduction to the Sociology of Music*, New York, Seabury Press, 1967, especially his foolish remarks about jazz. A more sympathetic approach to pop music can be found in Stith Bennett, *On Becoming a Rock Musician*, Amherst, University of Massachusetts Press, 1980.

2. Two superb examples are A. B. Spellman, *Black Music: Four Lives*, New York, Schocken Books, 1966; and Archie Green, *Only a Miner*, Champaign-Urbana, University of Illinois Press, 1972.

3. The New York weekly *The Village Voice* is one of the few periodicals that consistently discusses many styles of new music.

MUSIC AS A PART TIME PROFESSION

1. Robert A. Gorman, *The Recording Musician and Union Power: A Case Study of the American Federation of Musicians*, Washington D.C.: June 1978. This is Gorman's testimony before the Subcommittee on Courts, Civil Liberties, and the Administration of Justice of the Committee on the Judiciary, House of Representatives, Ninety-fifth Congress, Second Session. The figures given on page 1101 are for 1955. I suspect the situation is even worse today.

2. Robert R. Faulkner, *Hollywood Studio Musicians: Their Work and Careers in the Recording Industry*, Chicago, Aldine-Atherton, 1971. This is a superb sociological study of recording musicians.

3. Ross Russell, *Jazz Style in Kansas City and the Southwest*, Berkeley, University of California Press, 1971, p. 257.

4. Mary Flower is a friend of mine. The information in this article represents conversations over the last few years and an interview in August 1981.

5. Wesley Westbrooks, "Nothing Has Changed but the Tempo," in *The Folk Music Sourcebook*, by Larry Sandberg and Dick Weissman, New York, Alfred A. Knopf, 1976, pp. 34–6.

6. The author has received a grant from the National Endowment for the Humanities to write a book about Wesley Westbrooks. This article includes a small portion of the research involved in writing that book.

CONFESSIONS OF AN UNREPENTANT BANJO PLAYER

1. Kenneth Allsop, *Hard Travellin'; The Hobo and His History*, New York, New American Library, 1967, pp. 297–98.

LIFE AND MUSIC OF THE AMERICAN COWBOY

1. Clark Stanley, *The Life and Adventures of the American Cowboy: Life in the Far West*. Self-published, 1897.

2. N. Howard Tharp, *Songs of the Cowboys*. Self-published, Estancia, New Mexico, 1908.

3. John A. Lomax, *Cowboy Songs and Other Frontier Ballads*, New York, Macmillan, 1910.

4. Guy Logsdon, "The Cowboy's Bawdy Music," in Charles W. Harris and Buck Rainey, eds., *The Cowboy—Six Shooters, Songs, and Sex*, Norman, Okla., 1976, pp. 127–38.

5. J. Frank Dobie, *Texas and Southwestern Lore*, Dallas, SMU Press, 1967, facsimile edition, p. 155.

6. All songs mentioned, unless otherwise specified, can be found in John A. Lomax and Alan Lomax, *Cowboy Songs*, New York, Macmillan, 1941.

7. Pete Knight was a modern Canadian cowboy. Several songs have been written about his death. (See footnote 11.)

8. As sung by Harry Tuft, Denver, Colorado.

9. Austin and Alta Fife, *Saints of Saddle and Sage*, Bloomington, University of Indiana Press, 1956.

10. Ibid.

11. Glenn Ohrlin, *The Hellbound Train: A Cowboy Songbook*, Urbana, University of Illinois Press, 1973.

12. Gail I. Gardner, *Orejuna Bill*, self-published, Prescott, Arizona, 1950 reproduction edition.

13. Margaret Larkin, *The Singing Cowboy*, New York, Oak Publications, reprint, 1963.

14. N. Howard Tharp, *Song of the Cowboy*, ed. by Austin E. and Alta Fife, New York, Clarkson Potter, 1966.

15. The late Rogers was the dean of the University of Colorado Law School. An endless search for the town of Delores is chronicled in Katie Lee's *Ten Thousand Goddamned Cattle*, Flagstaff, Arizona, Northland Press, 1976.

16. Frummox, *From Here to There*, ABC Probe Records, CPLP 4511 S.

17. Mary McCaslin, *Way Out West*, Philo LP 1011.

18. Utah Phillips, Philo LP 1011.

19. William W. Savage Jr., *The Cowboy Hero*, Norman, University of Oklahoma Press 1979.

20. Jane Kramer, *The Last Cowboy*, New York, Harper & Row, 1977.

136   NOTES

21. Ivan Daines, *There's Something 'Bout a Rodeo*, Westmount Records, WSTM LP 7601. See the song "Silver Spurs."
22. Written by Ian Tyson and recorded by Ian and Sylvia, Judy Collins, and others.
23. See the folk song "The Wagoner's Lad," the pop song "The Wayward Wind," the blues song by Furry Lewis "Turn Your Money Green," etc.
24. Lew London, *Swingtime in Springtime*, Philo LP 1032.
25. Phillip Durham and Everett L. Jones, *The Negro Cowboys*, New York, Dodd, Mead & Co., 1965. On p. 3 they claim that there were some 5,000 black cowboys.
26. John A. Lomax, "Unexplored Treasures of Texas Folk-Lore," in Stith Thompson, ed., *Round the Levee*, Austin, Texas Folk-Lore Society Publications #1, 1916, p. 101.
27. John A. Lomax and Alan Lomax, op. cit., pp. 37–40, 420–21.
28. Ibid, p. 78.
29. E. C. Abbott and Helena Huntington Smith, *We Pointed Them North*, Norman, University of Oklahoma Press, 1954, pp. 224–29.
30. S. J. Sackett and William E. Koch, eds., *Kansas Folklore*, Lincoln, University of Nebraska Press, 1961.
31. Abbott and Smith, op. cit., pp. 228–29.
32. Information supplied by Paul Stewart, curator of the museum.
33. Durham and Jones, op. cit., mention black fiddlers, banjoists, and other musicians on pp. 50, 85, 105, 136, and 154. Stanley Vestal, *Queen of Cowtowns*, Lincoln, University of Nebraska Press, 1972, mentions black female piano players and singers on p. 229.

THE CONTEMPORARY MUSIC EDUCATOR

1. Max Kaplan, *Foundations and Frontiers of Music Education*, New York, Holt, Rinehart & Winston, 1966, p. 52.
2. Jacques Barzun, *Music in American Life*, Bloomington, Ind., Indiana University Press, comments on pp. 55–6 on the views of Paul Henry Lang, the noted musicologist.
3. Ruth Edwards, *The Compleat Music Teacher*, Los Angeles: Germ-X, Inc., 1970, p. 6.
4. Michael Mark, *Contemporary Music Education*, New York, Schirmer Books, 1978, p. 136.
5. Frigyes Sandor, ed., *Music Education in Hungary*, London, Boosey & Hawkes, 1969.
6. Theodore Tellstrom, *Music in American Education*, New York, Holt, Rinehart & Winston, 1971, p. 58.
7. Graham Vulliamy and Ed Lee, eds., *Pop Music in School*, Cambridge, England, Cambridge University Press, 2nd ed., 1980.
8. Malcolm Nicholls, "Running an 'Open' Music Department", in Vulliamy and Lee, p. 124.
9. Christopher Small, *Music · Society · Education*, New York, Schirmer Books, 1977, p. 172.
10. Thomas H. Carpenter, *Televised Music Instruction*, Washington, D.C., Music Educators National Conference, 1973, p. 108.

MUZAK AND THE LISTENER

1. Joyce Wadler, *Read about Muzak's Urban Squall Fame*, Denver Post, November 30, 1980.
2. David Pichaske, *A Generation in Motion: Popular Music and Culture of the Sixties*, New York, Schirmer Books, 1979, pp. 164–65.
3. R. Murray Schafer, *The Tuning of the World*, New York, Alfred Knopf, 1977, p. 96.
4. Ibid., p. 98.

THE MUSICIANS' UNION IN THE 1980S

1. Robert A. Gorman, "The Recording Musician and Union Power: A Case Study of the American Federation of Musicians," in *Performance Rights and Sound Recordings*, Subcommittee on Courts, Civil Liberties and the Administration of Justice of the Committee on the Judiciary, House of Representatives, Ninety-fifth Congress, Second Session, June 1978. Washington, D.C., U.S. Government Printing Office, 1978, p. 1075.

2. Robert D. Leiter, *The Musicians and Petrillo*, New York, Bookman Associates, 1953, p. 67.

3. Cecil Read, Statement of Cecil F. Read Before the Copyright Office, Library of Congress, July 28, 1977, Los Angeles, California, in *Performance Rights and Sound Recordings*, p. 652.

4. Victor W. Fuentealba, Letter to All AFM Recording Musicians, August 1, 1981.

5. *Annual Report, 1981:* Eighty-fourth Annual Convention of the American Federation of Musicians of the United States and Canada, Salt Lake City, June 25, 1981. Secretary-Treasurer's Report, p. 16.

6. Ibid, p. 15.

7. Ibid, p. 19.

THE ARTIST AND THE AUDIENCE

1. Christopher Small, *Music · Society · Education*, New York, Schirmer Books, 1977, p. 38.

2. Murray Schafer, *The Tuning of the World*, New York, Alfred A. Knopf, 1977, p. 7.

3. Alphonse Silbermann, *The Sociology of Music*, trans. by Corbet Stewart, London, Routledge & Kegan Paul, 1963, p. 31.

4. Kurt Wolf, trans., *The Sociology of George Simmel*, New York, Free Press of Glencoe, 1950, p. 342.

5. Jean Duvignaud, *The Sociology of Art*, trans. by Timothy Wilson, New York, Harper & Row, 1972, p. 141.

6. Herbert Read, *To Hell with Culture*, New York, Schocken Books, 1963, p. XI.

7. Tom Wolfe, *The Painted Word*, New York, Bantam Books, 1980, p. 4.

8. H. Stith Bennett, *On Becoming a Rock Musician*, Amherst, Mass., University of Massachusetts Press, 1980, pp. 7, 82, etc.

9. Small, op. cit., p. 160.

10. Jon Vriden Shepherd, et. al., *Whose Music? A Sociology of Musical Languages*, New Brunswick, N.J., Transaction Books, 1977; see Trevor Wishart, "On Radical Culture," pp. 243–44.

11. Sidney Finkelstein, *How Music Expresses Ideas*, New York, International Publishers, revised and enlarged edition, 1970, pp. 68–9.

12. Shepherd, et. al., op. cit., article by Graham Vulliamy, "Music and the Mass Culture Debate," p. 182.

13. Howard S. Becker, *Outsiders: Studies in the Sociology of Deviance*, New York, The Free Press, 1963, p. 89.

RECOMMENDED READING

The books listed below concern various aspects of music making in America. Some of them are cited as references in various chapters of this book, and others are simply books that I have found to be stimulating and enjoyable.

Abrahams, Roger. *Positively Black*. New York: Prentice Hall, 1970. Abrahams is a widely published folklorist, and this particular book is an interpretation of contemporary black culture through folklore and music.

Arian, Edward. *Bach, Beethoven and Bureaucracy: The Case of the Philadelphia Orchestra*. University, Alabama: University of Alabama Press, 1971. An ex-musician turned social scientist takes a tough and informed look at his musical alma mater.

Bennett, H. Stith. *On Becoming a Rock Musician*, Amherst, Mass.: University of Massachusetts Press, 1980. Sociologists may find the musical jargon hard to follow, and musicians will certainly find the sociological analysis tough going, but a worthwhile book, if for no other reason than the fact that Bennett examines the life of the working musician, not the superstar.

Burns, Joan Simpson. *The Awkward Embrace*. New York: Alfred A. Knopf, 1975. An examination of power in the arts.

Chapple, Steve and Garafalo, Reebee. *Rock 'n' Roll Is Here To Pay*.

Chicago: Nelson Hall, 1977. A radical critique of the rock record ratrace.

Drinker, Sophie. *Music and Women.* New York: Coward McCann, 1948. A pioneering book on the repression of women's roles and contributions throughout the history of music.

Faulkner, Robert R. *Hollywood Studio Musicians: Their Work and Careers in the Recording Industry.* Chicago: Aldine Atherton, 1971. A marvelous study of the world of the studio musician.

Galanoy, Terry, *Down the Tube.* New York: Pinnacle Books, 1972. A very amusing book about the making of television commercials.

Green, Archie. *Only a Miner.* Champaign, Illinois: University of Illinois Press, 1972. A marvelous book, about mining songs, integrating music with a variety of social science disciplines.

Greene, Bob. *The Billion Dollar Baby.* New York: Signet, 1974. A perceptive study of the selling of Alice Cooper by the well-known newspaper columnist.

Guralnick, Peter. *Feel Like Going Home.* New York: Outerbridge, 1971. Guralnick is one of the few writers whose interviews and commentary always seem to get to the heart of the matter. He writes about popular music with a true knowledge of its roots. His later book, *Lost Highway,* is equally enjoyable.

Hemphill, Paul. *The Nashville Sound: Bright Lights and Country Music.* New York: Pocket Books, 1971. An intelligent and well-written guide to the country music business.

Kramer, Jane. *The Last Cowboy.* New York: Harper and Row, 1977. An examination of the life and values of the modern American cowboy.

Nancy, Charles, Ed. *American Music from Storyville to Woodstock.* New Brunswick, New Jersey: Transaction Books, 1975. A collection of articles about rock and jazz of varying interest.

Hart, Philip. *Orpheus in the New World.* New York: W. W. Norton, 1973. A comprehensive and intelligent examination of the American symphony orchestra.

Schafer, R. Murry. *The Tuning of the World.* New York: Alfred A. Knopf, 1977. A thought-provoking and sensitive book by the Canadian composer and music educator.

Shapiro, Nat and Hentoff, Nat, Eds. *Hear Me Talkin' To Ya: The Story of Jazz by the Men Who Made It.* New York: Dover, 1966. For once, an accurately titled book. A series of interviews with various jazzmen.

Small, Christopher. *Music. Society. Education.* New York: Schirmer Books, 1977. An exciting book, full of thoughtful insights and interesting ideas. Highly recommended.

Southern, Eileen. *The Music of Black Americans.* New York: W. W. Norton, 1971. Essential reading.

Spellman, A. B. *Black Music: Four Lives.* New York: Schocken Books, 1970. A profoundly depressing book about four innovative modern jazz musicians.

Stokes, Geoffrey. *Star-Making Machinery: The Odyssey of an Album.* Indianapolis: Bobbs-Merrill, 1976. A fine book about the recording of popular music, and the drive for success.

Vulliamy, Graham and Lee, Ed, Eds. *Pop Music in School.* Cambridge, England, Cambridge University Press, 2nd Edition, 1980. A book full of innovative educational ideas.

INDEX